3-19

THE HOWDUNIT SERIES

AMATEUR DETECTIVES

a writer's guide to how private citizens solve criminal cases

D1052876

**ELAINE RACO CHASE
& ANNE WINGATE PH.D.**

WRITER'S DIGEST BOOKS
CINCINNATI, OHIO

Other fine Writer's Digest Books are available from your local bookstore or direct from the publisher.

00 99 98 97 96   5 4 3 2 1

Library of Congress Cataloging-in-Publication Data

Chase, Elaine Raco
    Amateur detectives / by Elaine Raco Chase and Anne Wingate.
        p.   cm.—(The Howdunit series)
    Includes bibliographical references and index.
    ISBN 0-89879-725-X (alk. paper)
    1. Detective and mystery stories—Authorship. I. Wingate, Anne. II. Title.
III. Series.
PN3377.5.D4C55   1996
808.3'872—dc20   96-33987
                                                                          CIP

Edited by Roseann Biederman
Cover designed by Leslie Meaux-Druly and Angela Lennert Wilcox
Cover illustration by Chris Spollen, Moonlightpress Studio

Dedication

Anne Wingate would like to dedicate her part of this book to Mary Ann Makaya, because she's such a wonderful friend.

Elaine Raco Chase would like to dedicate her part of this book to her son Marc, because he's going to make a wonderful detective.

Acknowledgments

Thanks to those of the states attorneys general who generously provided information; thanks to the University of Utah Law Library for having on hand the reference books for the states that didn't send information. A special thank you to the office of the Attorney General of Florida, which provided a complete list of the attorneys general of all of the United States and its possessions and territories.

We'd like to express our gratitude to the over two hundred authors, librarians, booksellers and fans who contributed their views on the popularity of the amateur sleuth mystery and their favorite sleuths. We've incorporated their incisive comments wherever possible.

A special thank you to: Carolyn G. Hart, Christina Carter, Anne Reisser and stalwart Nancy Drew fan, *Donna*, for their help and invaluable input.

—The Authors

Table of Contents

Introduction

As hard as it may be to believe, all detective work was amateur as recently as two hundred years ago. Although judges, sheriffs and constables existed, none of them had any real training in law enforcement. Anything stolen was probably gone for good. Murder might lead to an arrest and a hanging, or it might lead to a blood feud that could last for centuries. This means that the unwritten history of real amateur detectives is probably just about as long as the history, written and unwritten, of humanity.

In fiction and literature, the amateur detective has a respectable lineage, starting with an eighteenth dynasty Egyptian novel about one Sinuhe who had discovered a terrible secret involving the Pharaoh and was forced to flee as a result of it. There are numerous manuscript fragments of *The Tale of Sinuhe* but no complete copy. A number of years ago, Mika Waltari based his superb novel *The Egyptian* on the fragments.

Although Edgar Allan Poe is considered the "father of the detective story," the detective story had a long and respectable lineage before Poe was ever born. In fact, the mystery can be considered the primordial literature of humanity, helping to answer the primordial questions of humanity: Who am I? How did I get here? What am I doing here? Where am I going?

In fiction and in fact, many an amateur detective has been known to say something like this: "Solving crimes is something I'm more than happy to leave to the professionals." But sometimes in fact, and often in fiction, the professionals aren't quite able to do the job.

In fiction and in fact, many a police officer coping with a would-be amateur sleuth has been known to say something like this: "I knew she/he was going to be a problem. Too damn smart. Too much the busybody."

In fiction and in fact, amateur detectives are shrewd students of human nature. They possess keen insight and intellect. They are lively, energetic and curious risk-takers, no matter what their age or sex.

A special one-on-one relationship often forms between the reader and the character, so that the reader identifies with the character and—for the duration of the story—the reader mentally transforms into that feisty, witty, observant amateur.

But there are many problems in writing about—to say nothing of trying to be—an amateur sleuth. Some of the frequent questions from new writers are: "How do they handle the hostility of the police? Why do they always find the bodies? How can they hope to compete with the new crime scene technology that involves things like computers and DNA? Aren't amateur detective novels becoming passé?"

The last question has a fast answer: No, not at all. In fact, they are increasing in both number and popularity. Writers are scouring the pages of history to give us sleuths in ancient Rome, ancient Egypt, medieval Europe and just about anywhere else and anytime else that anybody can think of.

Mystery readers can be found in the White House (they helped FDR through World War II and President Bill Clinton is an avid fan) and in the poor house (more than a few homeless people forget their troubles in the pages of a good mystery).

Who are the favorite amateur detectives of all time? We asked writers, readers, librarians and academics to give us their opinions. We received over two hundred responses—the overwhelming favorite listing was Dorothy L. Sayers' Lord Peter Wimsey, who was followed closely by Nancy Drew and Agatha Christie's Miss Jane Marple. The most popular favorites today are: Carolyn G. Hart's Annie Laurance Darling, Margaret Maron's Judge Deborah Knot, Nancy Pickard's Jenny Cain and Elizabeth Peters' Amelia Peabody.

This list appears biased toward female intuition, but the reason is that a higher percentage of mysteries intended for largely male audiences feature law enforcement professionals rather than amateur sleuths. In fact, most of the few male amateurs, except (perhaps) the Hardy Boys, are written for and by women.

The basic plot of mystery fiction moves either from order to disorder to order to disorder to order; which one depends on what point in the case the story begins. Almost all detective novels provide a satisfying read in which good triumphs over evil with all the loose ends tied up. In particular, the amateur detective story leaves the reader with the pleasant glow of feeling, "Well, I could do that too if I were ever in such a situation and I really tried."

As a writer, you must think up and discover who your fictional amateur detective is going to be, what his or her characteristics are going to be, how you are going to make your story or novel work, how your detective is going to get information and, at least equally important, how *you* are going to get the information you need to make your mystery work.

This book should guide you, give you many ideas and help you figure out how to make those ideas work and come together to create a captivating amateur detective novel.

Good writing! We hope you enjoy *Amateur Detectives*. We look forward to reading yours.

The Authors

The History of the Amateur Detective Novel

What a Writer Needs to Know

Writers are often told: "Write what you know." To be a writer of the amateur sleuth mystery novel, you need to know and study the traditions and history of the genre. A writer should learn about the climate of the times and how real history brought about and impacted the amateur detective novel.

To be an effective and powerful writer, no matter what genre of writing you pursue, you must immerse yourself in both the popular and not-so-popular works of the past and present. Our first piece of advice is to read as much of the genre as you can. The great masters will prove to be excellent teachers and save you a great deal of trial-and-error time. We are not suggesting that you force your writing to mimic another author's style, but to use the books as learning tools—as if they were textbooks. This is not to say a writer should not experiment and expand on the amateur sleuth novel. A writer learns and hones the craft of writing by *pushing the envelope*. As you read the mystery novels of the past, you will discover that these talented writers did push the envelope, which is why their amateur sleuths are still being reprinted by publishers today.

It is especially important for the writer of amateur sleuth fiction to study the genre because there are so few real-life amateur detectives to draw on. By studying the novels, you can see how other writers have handled such obstacles inherent in the genre as: How the amateur continually becomes involved in murders; what jobs give an amateur access to cases and the freedom to solve them; how the amateur finds information about suspects when they do not have access to official law enforcement databases and other technology.

This chapter will introduce you to the great amateur sleuths of the past, help guide your reading and supply you with a firm foundation of the genre. We will also provide you with an overview of the history of law enforcement and its relevance to the history of the times. We have organized the classic sleuths by profession and with dates of publication as an extra reference.

A Brief History of Law Enforcement

The idea of law enforcement as protection to society developed from the use of the military as guardians of the peace. In 27 B.C., Roman Emperor Augustus extended the Praetorian Guard by forming a nonmilitary force called the *vigiles*. Augustus divided the vigiles into nine *cohorts* (groups) of a thousand men each. Three of the cohorts remained in Rome while the others were stationed in nearby cities. The Romans achieved a high level of law enforcement that lasted until the decline of the empire and the beginning of the Middle Ages.

In the fifth century, law enforcement became the function of the heads of fiefdoms and principalities. In England, policing became the responsibility of the nobles on their individual estates. When a serious crime occurred, all able-bodied men joined in the chase of the suspect. The suspect was then brought before the *shire reeve* or county chief. The word *sheriff* is the shortened form of shire reeve.

Later, each noble appointed a *constable* to keep the peace and arrest and guard criminals. For decades, constables were unpaid citizens who took turns at the unpopular job. By the mid-sixteenth century, wealthy citizens began paying people to become constables. As more and more constables became paid, the quality of their work declined.

In 1663, officials in London began paying old men to guard the streets at night. Until the end of the eighteenth century, these inefficient *watchmen* and the constables were the only form of police in the city. The people, however, demanded a more effective force to protect them and to deal with criminals.

In 1750, Henry Fielding, a London magistrate and author, organized a group of law officers called the *Bow Street Runners*. They would run to the scene of the crime, capture the criminal and begin an investigation. What happened if the criminal did not stick around to be captured? The principle technique of the police was to rely on other criminal informants as eyewitnesses. Early criminal investigation was crude and confessions were often extracted under torture. It was only in recent times that science and scientific facts entered the picture.

British statesman Sir Robert Peel, under instructions from Parliament in 1829, established the London Metropolitan Police, which became the world's first organized police force and the basis for Scotland Yard. The British influenced the development of criminal investigation in the United States.

The American colonists used the English watch system in the towns and villages of New England. In the southern colonies, sheriffs kept the peace. As Americans moved West, sheriffs and marshals tried to preserve the peace across the vast territory. But quite often citizens formed groups of self-appointed law officers called *vigilantes* to capture and immediately punish outlaws by way of hanging.

In 1845, both New York City and Boston combined its separate day and night watches into a single police force patterned after Scotland Yard, not only in response to crime but to control citizen unrest. Soon other American cities formed similar police departments.

Those early police departments were poorly organized; the officers were underpaid and received little or no training. Bribery and corruption were high at all levels of government. The heads of the powerful political machines controlled the city leaders and police, using them to intimidate political opponents or for other corrupt personal services.

During the late 1800s and early 1900s, a strong spirit of reform swept across an ever-growing urban America. The impersonal fast-paced city life led to a rise in juvenile delinquency, crime and antisocial behavior. In the early 1900s, August Vollmer, the police chief of Berkeley, California, gained fame as a reformer. He urged reorganization of the departments, college education for officers and the use of scientific methods in police work.

While conservatives were calling for a return to law and order, the majority of the population didn't seem bothered by even more corruption and scandals at all levels of government. Popular entertainment featured the slapstick action of the silent movie's Keystone Kops. Between 1910 and 1929, producer Mack Sennett didn't help the image of police by producing over one thousand movies where the bumbling Kops seldom arrested anyone but if they did, it always turned out to be the wrong person.

In 1920, Congress passed the 18th Amendment calling for prohibition of alcoholic beverages. Underworld gangs flourished as they provided many law-abiding citizens with bootleg liquor. Bank robberies, kidnappings and other violent crimes broke out during the twenties and thirties. A large percentage of police officers and police departments were *on the take* and received money to look the other way as gangsters became the behind-the-scenes rulers of the cities.

With such a negative image of the police and public officials along with a history of citizen involvement in law enforcement, how could the idea of an amateur detective not be conceived? The amateur was greatly needed, especially one who was intelligent, honest, clever, resourceful and incorruptible—all the attributes that were obviously lacking in those of authority.

The First Amateur Sleuth

The first amateur detective arrived as a poor medical student who loved books. **Chevalier Auguste Dupin** was Edgar Allan Poe's cerebral hero who had astounding powers of observation and applied rigorous logic to solve crimes. Poe was a student of French writer Francois Voltaire and especially liked his longest story, *Zadig*, or *The Mystery of Fate*. Dupin mirrored Zadig in that they were both "as wise as possible for a man to be," highly educated, especially in the sciences, and knew all that was known about human nature. Dupin was a rationalist who felt that everything could be explained and expressed in mathematical formulas.

Poe was able to voice his views on many subjects using his character Dupin as the narrator of these stories. Poe denied the supernatural and focused on scientific analysis. Through author Poe, amateur sleuth Dupin was able to match and identify his intellect with that of the villain ("I kill, therefore, I am"). Over and over, Dupin mirrored creator Poe as he dedicated himself to studying all trivial details that deviated from the norm and solved puzzles and cryptograms by working them backwards.

Dupin made his debut in 1841 in "The Murders in the Rue Morgue." That was followed by "The Mystery of Marie Rogêt" in 1842, which was based on the unsolved murder of a woman in Hoboken, New Jersey, and "The Purloined Letter" in 1845.

Dupin blazed the trail for a variety of fictional detectives, be they amateur, private or police. For the writers of the day, amateur detectives started to appear in the most unusual places and with quite varied backgrounds.

Jacks- and Jills-of-All-Trades

Anna Katherine Green, the first woman to publish a detective novel, became known as the "mother" of the genre, having penned *The Leavenworth Case* in 1878 and becoming the first woman to have published a detective novel. While the hero of this piece was police officer **Ebenezer Gryce**, Anna did write other mystery novels featuring Gryce's two office workers, **Violet Strange** and **Amelia Butterworth**. Amelia is used by her employer to gain information from people in upper society.

George R. Sims' **Sir Arthur Strangeways** (1890) gets into many harrowing situations from playing detective when he answers personal ads as in *The Case of George Candlemas*. A.A. Milne, of Winnie-the-Pooh fame, created the zany **Anthony**

"Madman" Gillingham in 1922 in *The Red House Mystery.* Milne, who edited a humor magazine and wrote many comic essays, created what became known as the "what fun comic" amateur detective novel.

Bill Parmelee (1928) is a cardsharp who solves gambling mysteries in Percival Wilde's novel, *Rogues in Clover.* Vincent Starrett's **Walter Ghost** (1929) is an amateur who can solve crimes aboard cruise ships just by reading cablegrams in *Murder on "B" Deck.*

"Common sense" was Cape Cod handyman **Asey Mayo**'s trademark. Phoebe Atwood Taylor's sailor solved the first of many mysteries in 1931's *The Cape Cod Mystery.* If you need a crime solved and a coat mended, head for London's West End and ask for Valentine Williams' **Mr. Treadgold** (1936), who first appeared in *Dead Man Manor.* But if you're interested in an amateur who can solve crimes without wearing a stitch, take a peek at **Gypsy Rose Lee.** Craig Rice penned the *G-String Murders* in 1941 for the famed stripper.

All **Mr. Mycroft** wanted was peace and quiet for himself and lots of honey from his bees. However, his retirement to Sussex in 1941's *A Taste for Honey* proved to be filled with crimes to solve courtesy of author H.F. Heard. Peace and quiet were hardly the life that **Ed** and **Ambrose Hunter** (1947) led. Frederic Brown's carnival workers became professional private eyes after solving a few crimes as amateurs. *The Fabulous Clipjoint* was Brown's first mystery (which won him an Edgar Award), and Ed and Am's first appearance as amateur sleuths.

James Yaffer provided readers with the "mother" of all amateurs in the person of **Mom.** She's a Jewish widow who lives in the Bronx (1952). While serving Friday night supper to her son the police detective, Mom manages to solve all his tough cases just by listening and adding her common sense as in *Mom Knows Best.*

Buoyed by countless cups of Turkish coffee to get him through his twenty-hour days, **Pierre Chambrun** managed one of New York's luxurious hotels, The Beaumont, in 1962. Judson Philips writing as Hugh Pentecost has the French immigrant solving any and all crimes that threaten to damage the famed hotel's reputation. Chambrun made his first appearance in *The Cannibal Who Overate*.

One of the most highly regarded *jack-of-all-trades* has to be John D. MacDonald's **Travis McGee**. Although he simply bills himself as a recoverer of stolen property, Travis proves to be a private avenger and saintlike knight-errant when it comes to righting wrongs. McGee calls home, *The Busted Flush*, which is docked in Ft. Lauderdale and made his debut in 1964's *The Deep Blue Good-By*.

Ross Thomas, writing as Oliver Bleeck, created his knight-errant in the persona of **Philip St. Ives**. St. Ives is a paid helper who gets back stolen objects or retrieves kidnapped people as the title of his first book *The Brass Go-Between* (1969) aptly suggests.

"I Know All and See All and Solve All"

M.P. Shiel created the exiled Russian nobleman, **Prince Zaleski** (1895), in *Prince Zaleski*. Author Shiel proved to be as arrogant as Zaleski when he christened his character as the "legitimate son of Edgar Allen Poe's Dupin and Sherlock Holmes as Poe's bastard son." The prince solved crimes while in a drug-induced state from the comfort of his London flat.

Drugs weren't needed by *The Thinking Machine*. Jacques Futrelle created **Professor Augustus S.F.X. Van Dusen** in 1906's *The Diamond Master*. The diminutive professor with a huge head taught at a college in Boston and readily demonstrated how easy it was to use logic and intellect to solve crimes even if totally unfamiliar with the facts.

If there's a scent of garlic in the air and the room is filled with candles and jars of water, **Carnacki** is on the case. William Hope Hodgson's psychic (1910) was always ready to explain how the so-called supernatural crime was quite ordinary as in *Carnacki, The Ghost-Finder*. When Scotland Yard was really baffled, Edgar Wallace's "psychometrical" **Derrick Yale** (1922) stands ready to solve the case as in *The Crimson Circle*; as does Carolyn Well's **Pennington Wise**, psychic investigator (1942).

Philip MacDonald penned the adventures of seer **Dr. Alcazar** in 1930. Nine years later, **The Great Merlini** retired from the circus and opened a magic store in Times Square. Clayton Rawson had his magician and seer help New York City's police solve many a baffling case in 1940's *The Headless Lady.*

Step Up to the Bar

Lawyers have appeared as amateur detectives in many novels but not always on the side of the law. One of the earliest was Melville Davisson Post's **Randolph Mason** (1896). Mason was more amoral rogue than officer of the court. In *The Corpus Delicti*, Mason advises his client how to kill his wife and get away with murder by adhering to the stated letter of the law. All the cases were based on actual trials and legal loopholes, which caused concern among jurists that Post's fictional writings would serve as a handbook for criminals. Post's stories actually brought about change to the criminal justice system. Soon Randolph Mason began working for the law rather than the criminals in his later adventures.

Louis Tracy's **Reginald Brett** was a London barrister who worked for the court by solving *The Albert Gate Mystery* in 1904. Here in the United States, Arthur Train created a lawyer who never lost a case, wasn't concerned with charging a fee and was born on the Fourth of July. Too good to be true? No, he's **Ephraim Tutt** of Pottsville, New York, who began his legal life in 1919 with *Mock Hen and Mock Turtle*. Tutt, like Sherlock Holmes, became so real to readers that they refused to believe he was a fictional character.

Baroness Orczy's shyster lawyer, **Patrick Mulligan** (1928), doesn't mind going to the extremes to get a client off as well as solve the crime. Although shyster barrister **Joshua Clunk** handled the criminal woes of the underworld, he does find time to help Scotland Yard in twelve novels by H.C. Bailey beginning with 1930's *The Garston Murder Case.*

He may be the most famous attorney in fiction. He's never lost a client or a case (okay, there was that *Terrified Typist Case* but the client was bogus) much to the aggravation of District Attorney Hamilton Burger. His secretary and paramour, Della Street, knows he's a man who can be trusted and she does, quite often, with her life. He's Erle Stanley Gardner's **Perry Mason,** who began his career of over eighty cases in 1933 by solving *The Case of the Velvet Claws*. Mason, like his creator, possessed a sharp legal mind that used many "courtroom theatrics" to ferret out the real murderer.

His British counterpart would have to be **Arthur Crook**, Anthony Gilbert's famed barrister of over fifty novels. Crook appeared in 1936 and, like Perry Mason, always uncovered the true murderer of the crime to save his client.

One of the few prosecutors to go the extra mile to ferret out the truth, **Doug Selby** made sure he brought the right criminal to justice as district attorney of Madison County, California. Erle Stanley Gardner created Selby in 1937 in *The DA Calls It Murder*.

Craig Rice's Chicago lawyer, **John J. Malone** (1939), liked whiskey more than the law but managed to find the true killer and save his clients. Aging and rather unsuccessful as a lawyer, Cyril Hare's **Francis Pettigrew** (1946) was sharp-witted enough to unravel the most baffling case. Harold Q. Masur's **Scott Jordan** (1947) does his lawyering out of a hotel in New York City, while shrewd attorney **"Uncle" Gavin Stevens** holds court in William Faulkner's Yoknapatawpha County in the 1948 novel *Intruder in the Dust*.

In 1949, Robert Van Gulik used actual historical cases as the background for the famous Chinese **Judge Dee**. Set in 660 China, Dee is based on statesman Ti Jen-chieh of the T'ang Dynasty. In over eighteen books, beginning with *The Chinese Bell Murders*, Judge Dee, along with his three wives and sons, travels among the common people to investigate crimes.

Sara Wood's **Antony Maitland**, the famed English barrister, hung out his shingle in 1962's *Bloody Instructions*. Maitland, a former World War II British secret agent, used skilled cross-examination of witnesses to prove the innocence of his clients in over twenty novels.

When They Were Good, They Were Very, Very Good. When They Were Bad, They Were Even Better

Mystery novels deal with people ranging from petty thieves to murderers, blackmailers to kidnappers, robbers with guns to robbers with computers. In the late 1890s swindling was a popular game, along with gamblers (both male and female), bookmakers and *gentlemen* crooks. Today's writers prefer to call such characters *antiheroes*—bad guys with a penchant for doing good. There are, of course, limits to how *bad* an author can make their sleuth without losing the sympathies of the reader.

In 1897, author Grant Allen created one such gentleman crook in **Colonel Clay**. Clay made Sir Charles Vandrift in *An African Millionaire* his personal victim. Vandrift, who made his millions in illegal African trade, was constantly duped, robbed, cheated and fooled by the many disguises of Colonel Clay. Guy Boothby's gentleman crook **Simon Carne** made his debut in 1899 in *A Prince of Swindlers*; followed in 1899 by E.W. Hornung's **A.J. Raffles**, who first appeared in *The Amateur Cracksman*. Hornung, Sir Arthur Conan Doyle's brother-in-law, agreed to write a series of mystery stories featuring a character totally opposite from the popular Sherlock Holmes. Raffles is presented as a *cricketer* (honorable scion) of a good family. After his family lost everything, he made his living from the daring robberies he indulged in whenever his funds ran low.

In 1907, Maurice LeBlanc reformed the Prince of Thieves, **Arsene Lupin**, and had him aid the French Sureté in *Les Trois Crimes d'Arsene Lupin*. O. Henry's **Jimmy Valentine** (1909) gave up being a burglar and safecracker to aid the police. In 1910, Scotland Yard called master criminal, **Hamilton Cleek**, "The Man of Forty Faces" because he was able to contort his face into a variety of disguises and get away with the most outrageous crimes. After marrying the lovely Ailsa, Cleek— created by author Thomas W. Hanshew—gave up his ill-gotten ways and helped fight injustice in *Cleek's Government Cases*.

A "Robin Hood" complex began to emerge among the rogue amateur detectives. **Smiler Bunn** was Bertram Atkey's (1911) portly, middle-aged crook who only stole from other crooks, making legal confrontation impossible in eleven novels that spanned over thirty years beginning with *The Amazing Mr. Bunn*. **Jimmie Dale**, the Gray Seal, dallied in New York City (the American version of Robin Hood's Sherwood Forest) in *The Adventures of Jimmie Dale*. Frank L. Packard's 1916 sophisticate belonged to all the exclusive clubs but commanded a gang of safecrackers that only committed illegal acts to correct injustices. The Gray Seal would soon find himself being black-mailed to go straight by a beautiful woman.

Jack Boyle's **Boston Blackie** was an ex-con and safe-cracker who prowled San Francisco in 1919. Author Boyle viewed Blackie as a skilled crook made even more dangerous because of his intellect. Blackie was a man who fought against society's injustices. While the hero of just one book, Boston Blackie became famous via TV, radio and movies. H.C. McNeile's **Bulldog Drummond** was an adventurer who found things a bit dull after World War I. In 1920, *Bulldog Drummond* was the first novel in a series that would span from the Roaring Twenties to the cold war of the late 1950s. The intensely patri-otic Drummond was derisive of the police and those who could manipulate the law, especially his main adversary, archvillain Carl Peterson.

Retired World War I military types flourished as amateur detectives. Philip MacDonald created **Anthony Gethryn** in 1924's *The Rasp* in which he's Scotland Yard's prime murder suspect. The ageless Gethryn's most famous and last adventure was *The List of the Adrian Messenger* (1959). She may have looked like an angel but she was the notorious gang leader, **Fidelity Dove**. The violet-eyed Ms. Dove had a devastating effect on most men but lived a strict puritanical lifestyle. Created by Roy Vickers in 1924's *The Exploits of Fidelity Dove*, Fidelity and her gang of lawyers, scientists and businessmen were advo-cates of those who could not help themselves and aggravated Scotland Yard.

By day, **Richard Verrell** was one of London's wealthy aristocrats. At night, you'd find him dressed all in black as one of the city's most artful safecrackers. Bruce Graeme's thief appeared in over a dozen novels beginning in 1925 with *Blackshirt*. **Blackshirt** soon found himself at the mercy of the fair Bobbie, who blackmailed him into a life of crime solving and marriage.

He was rich, handsome, elegant and never uneasy, no mat-ter what the situation. But once the bad guys saw his "stick-man" calling card, they fled in terror at the sign of **The Saint**. Leslie Charteris' **Simon Templar** was another modern-day Robin Hood who made life a living hell for poor Chief Inspector

Claude Eustace Teal of Scotland Yard beginning with *Meet the Tiger* (1928). His halo was never tarnished because he, too, corrected injustices and only robbed criminals.

If you wanted to know who had the evil heart, just ask **The Shadow** aka **Lamont Cranston**. Maxwell Grant's millionaire hero captured criminals using his hypnotic powers to "cloud men's minds." The Shadow even had his own pulp magazine; the first edition was published in 1931. The Shadow delighted radio listeners for many years.

Millionaire playboys leading double lives became the norm as amateur detectives. John Creasy introduced **The Toff, Honorable Richard Rollison**, in 1933. Then Creasy, using the pen name Anthony Morton, created **John Mannering, The Baron**, in 1937. Both The Toff and The Baron held court in London's Mayfair district. Both were respected gentlemen by day, with The Baron running an antique shop, but each used his safecracking and thieving skills to solve crimes for Scotland Yard. Michael Arlen added another "Robin Hood" to this collection when he introduced **The Falcon, Gay Stanhope Falcon**, to readers in the 1940 short story that inspired several movies.

Earl Drake, Dan J. Marlowe's "The Man With Nobody's Face," exploded on the printed page in 1962's *The Name of the Game Is Death* as a completely amoral criminal who shot his way out of jail and ended up helping right many a wrong.

The Roar of the Greasepaint, the Smell of Death

When her young artist husband went blind, English actress **Dorcas Dene** (1897) began solving crimes to make extra money in the George R. Sims' mystery novel bearing her name. Famous actor and London stage manager, **Sir John Saumarez**, solved crimes in 1928 for author Helen D. Simpson in *Enter Sir John*.

Elderly and deaf, **Drury Lane** made his appearance in 1932's *The Tragedy of X*. Ellery Queen had his wealthy former Shakespearean actor solve crimes from the comfort of his Hudson River mansion for the NYPD. From the very uncomfortable confines of a 1936 mental ward, **Peter Duluth** discovers he hasn't got time to have a complete nervous breakdown—there's a murder to be solved in *A Puzzle for Fools*. The alcoholic theatrical producer later marries fellow patient Iris Patterson and goes on to solve more theater-related crimes created by author Patrick Quentin. Carolyn Wells' silent screen movie star, **Kenneth Carlisle**, gives up his career to solve murders in 1939.

They're Not Getting Older—Just Better

You'll find him sitting quite comfortably in his chair in the corner of a London tea shop waiting for young reporter Polly Burton to visit. In 1901, Baroness Emmuska Orczy, who also created "The Scarlet Pimpernel" and "Lady Molly of Scotland Yard," wrote about **The Old Man in the Corner**. While he tied the most intricate of knots, the Old Man also solved the most complex crimes without ever leaving his chair in the corner.

In 1918, Melville Davisson Post penned the historical amateur, **Uncle Abner**. Abner was a country squire in Virginia's backwoods during Thomas Jefferson's presidency. Using Biblical knowledge and the ability to judge men's souls, Abner proved to be the *Master of Mysteries*, which was also the title of his debut novel.

She loved to help young lovers in trouble and even Scotland Yard called on her for help. Spinster **Miss Maud Silver** (1928) was a former governess who knitted and used pure logic to solve crimes in over thirty-two novels by Patricia Wentworth. Perhaps she'd have been a spinster no more if she would have left her cottage and visited Wales. That's where David Frome's widower, **Evan Pinkerton** (1930), turned up bodies.

The most noted spinster sleuth was St. Mary Mead's **Miss Jane Marple**. Dame Agatha Christie based Miss Marple on her Victorian grandmother. The eighty-something Miss Marple is portrayed as having a keen intellect and a shrewd nature that aids her in solving the most baffling crimes. Her first appearance was in 1930 in *Murder at the Vicarage*. Christie gifted us with more than a dozen Miss Marple mysteries over the years.

John Dickson Carr's **"Old Man" Sir Henry Merrivale** (1934) was skilled at solving locked room and supernatural crimes. Four years later, William Hulbert Footner patterned his

---

Editor Linda Hutton notes: "Miss Marple was without a doubt the greatest amateur sleuth because she seldom examined the scene of the crime, merely asked questions of eyewitnesses and made her deductions from them. Miss Marple never sought payment or thanks for her solutions, but when such came her way, she accepted them graciously."

---

amateur, **Amos Lee Mappin**, after Charles Dickens's Mr. Pickwick.

With her cat Samantha in her carrier, the globe-trotting **Miss Rachel Murdock** plied her amateur skills in D.B. Olsen's series. Miss Murdock first takes aim at a killer when her cat inherits a fortune in 1939's *The Cat Saw Murder.*

Is There a Doctor on the Case?

They probed and poked and, later, x-rayed. While doctors were amateur sleuths, they were quite the professionals when it came to solving crimes. Physicians relied on scientific clues and forensics rather than intuition or keen insight. Perhaps the greatest was **Dr. John Thorndyke** created by R. Austin Freeman in 1907 to solve the case of *The Red Thumb Mark.* Thorndyke was a forensic scientist and lawyer who always traveled with his green research kit. He approached each case with methodical detail and an absence of emotion. Thorndyke's address, 5A King's Bench Walk, became almost as famous as Sherlock Holmes' 221B Baker Street.

Author Freeman was himself interested in science, tried out his plots in his laboratory and used illustrations in his mystery novels. The English police were so impressed with Freeman and his sleuth Thorndyke that they adopted some of his scientific methods.

Freeman gave a new twist to the mystery genre by introducing the *inverted* story. This starts by describing the crime, gives the solution to the mystery and then goes on to reveal the work of detection. The inverted story allows the reader to study the villain, consider his state of mind and motives, then move on to concentrate on the sleuth and his deductive skills.

Psychological detective **Luther Trant** made his debut in 1909 from Edwin Balmer and William Macharg. Perhaps his "thought waves" were picked up by **Dr. Xavier Wycherly** in 1911 when Max Rittenberg created his psychological sleuth.

The "American Sherlock Holmes" appeared in 1912 from the pen of Arthur B. Reeve. Enter **Craig Kennedy**, professor of chemistry at Columbia University and predictor of such crime-fighting miracles as lie detectors and seismographs that could detect footsteps. Kennedy aided NYPD in twenty-six novels beginning with *The Silent Bullet*. Michael White's chemical criminologist, **Proteus Raymond** (1912), used radioactive saturnium rays to vaporize dead bodies.

In over twenty books, H.C. Bailey had his physician and surgeon, **Reginald Fortune**, advise Scotland Yard in a series of twenty-one novels that began with *Call Mr. Fortune* in 1920. The Yard also sought help from **Dr. Lancelot Priestley**, author and mathematician who used logic to solve crimes beginning in 1925 with *The Paddington Mystery* and continuing until 1961's *The Vanishing Diary*.

When you needed to focus on the female psyche, call William H. Footner's psychologist **Madame Rosika Storey** (1925), who would feed fruit tidbits to her pet monkey while she contemplated the case at hand. Need a specialist who knew the workings of the criminal mind? T.S. Stribling created **Professor Henry Poggiole, Ph.D.** in 1929. Unfortunately the Professor used the trial and error method of crime solving and wasn't always successful on the first try.

Mary Roberts Rinehart created the "had I but known" school of mystery novels. Her **Nurse Adams** knew quite a lot when it came to helping the police solve crimes; they called her "Miss Pinkerton" (1932).

If the crime was *impossible* with an aura of the supernatural, there was only one person who could be counted on to solve it. Who else but John Dickson Carr's giant **Dr. Gideon Fell**. In 1933 with *Hag's Nook*, followed by more than two dozen other mystery novels, Fell showed how the impossible was quite probable.

As medical assistant to the Manhattan D.A.'s office, **Dr. Basil Willing** (1938) was able to find "psychic fingerprints" and turn "lies into psychological facts" under the pen of Helen McCloy. As psychiatric consultant to the British Home Office, Gladys Mitchell's **Dame Beatrice Bradley** (1942) used the supernatural to help her solve cases.

Author Pele Plante notes: "Unlike Jane Marple, Dame Beatrice did not manipulate some male into doing her work for her. She was smooth and suave and quite unusual for her time, an older female Simon Templar."

Not only was medical missionary **Dr. Mary Finney** (1945) able to stop a native uprising in the Congo, she also solved a murder in Matthew Head's novel *The Devil in the Bush*. New York psychiatrist **Dr. Emmanuel Cellini** didn't travel quite that far to solve crimes. Kyle Hunt, one of John Creasy's many aliases, had him aid Scotland Yard with his intuitive mind. Even though she tried to retire to Arizona, pathologist **Dr. Grace Severance** found too many corpses to enjoy the desert in Margaret Scherf's 1968 novel, *The Banker's Bones*.

We'd be negligent not to mention that between 1930 and the 1950s, many authors were putting a scientific amateur detective in more of a science fiction venue than mystery. Authors created the future with amateurs who were able to change the color of people's skin, create artificial night, use hypnotic machines to find the truth, wear radio waves to shock villains, join forces with aliens to capture interplanetary criminals and even compete with a robot to solve crimes.

The Fourth Estate

Reporters and novelists make natural amateur detectives. Reporters are always hunting for information that could turn a routine story into a major headline. Novelists are natural detectives, researching their material and always finding more and more questions that need answers.

Gaston Leroux's **Joseph Rouletabille** (1907) was a young police reporter interested in finding out all the facts in *The Mystery of the Yellow Room*. Fleet Street crime journalist and artist **Philip Trent** was unable to stop himself from falling in love with a murder suspect. E.C. Bentley's Trent was more human than most as his solution to the murder in 1913's *Trent's Last Case* was wrong. British novelist and crime writer, **Roger Sheringham**, was quite vain over the fact he could solve most crimes. Author Anthony Berkeley, however, made Sheringham wrongly deduce the killer in *The Poisoned Chocolates Case* (1925).

He was quite handsome but rather arrogant as he helped his father, Inspector Richard Queen, solve over forty puzzlers. **Ellery Queen**, mystery author and rare book collector, first appeared in Ellery Queen's 1929 classic *The Roman Hat Mystery*. Both Ellerys were blessed with keen intellect, a cunning mind and stunning powers of observation.

St. John Sprigg's **Charles Venables** was a newspaper columnist who lived in a hotel where murder seemed a natural occurrence in 1933's *Pass the Body*. **Susan Dare** was a young mystery story writer who solved crimes in Mignon G. Eberhart's *The Cases of Susan Dare* (1934). Berkeley, California, is where mystery writer **Todd McKinnon** sought solutions to puzzling cases in Lenore Glen Offord's novel *Murder on Russian Hill* (1938).

New York bibliophile and author **Henry Gamadge** is often called upon to help a museum locate a missing rare manuscript or lost volume of poems. Gamadge debuts in Elizabeth Daly's 1940 novel *Unexpected Night*, which begins the fifteen-book series. Set in Chicago during the Roaring Twenties, Walter Starrett created antiquarian book dealer **Jimmie Lavender** in 1944.

She taught French, wrote a best-selling novel on psychology and easily solved crimes. She's Josephine Tey's **Miss Pym** (1946). Back in New York City, author David Alexander created **Bart Hardin**, editor of the fictional *Broadway Times*, who helps police solve crimes on *The Great White Way* (1954). He may have only one leg, but Judson Philips' **Peter Style** (1960) knows how to use his magazine column to crusade for justice and solve murders.

God Is Their Watson

Clerical amateurs seem to be more intent on saving souls and having criminals repent than putting them behind bars. In 1911, when G.K. Chesterton decided to pen mystery novels, I doubt he ever thought his **Father Brown** would be considered one of the three greatest detectives in literature—right up there with Sherlock Holmes and Dupin. In over fifty novels and without the help of the police, nonviolent Catholic priest Father Brown is able to use his humor and gentle ways to make the criminals change their violent ways.

Margaret Scherf's slow, plodding cleric **Martin Buell** (1948) finds life in Montana anything but dull in his series debut *Always Murder a Friend*. Buell's opposite would have to be burly **Father Joseph Bredder** of Los Angeles Franciscan Convent of the Holy Innocents. Leonard Holton created his ex-Marine sergeant and amateur boxer priest in 1959 and let him help his friend Lt. Minardi solve murders among the not-so-innocents in Los Angeles.

You'd expect life to be quieter in Barnard's Crossing, Massachusetts, but not with Harry Kemelman's **Rabbi David Small** around. Ever since *The Rabbi Slept Late* in 1964, David Small has been turning up bodies and solving crimes by looking at the "third side" of the question, which helps him aid Police Chief Hugh Lanigan.

What You See Isn't Always What You'll Get

Perhaps it was because of his exposé into the famous "patent medicine" quackery that made Samuel Hopkins Adams create an amateur detective who was an advertising director. In 1911, **Adrian Van Reypen Egerton** was more used to calling himself **Average Jones** and solving a series of highly unusual crimes that often had a medical background due to the author's journalistic writings. Hugh Pentecost's **Julian Quist** runs an advertising agency in his debut 1971 novel *Don't Drop Dead Tomorrow*. His foppish mannerisms cloak a sharp mind and tough manner that get one of his wealthy clients out of trouble when the need arises.

His resumé says he's a government chemist whose job is to test soil samples, but somehow Francis Lynde's **Calvin Sprague** (1912) finds himself solving some baffling crimes on board trains in *Scientific Sprague*. No doubt Sprague shared a vegetarian meal or two with Victor L. Whitechurch's **Thorpe**

Hazell (1912), who knew those railroad boxcars harbored many a mystery that needed solving in *Thrilling Stories of the Railway*.

When is the *Mona Lisa* not the *Mona Lisa*? When the painting is brought to **Joe Quinney** (1913). Horace A. Vachell's art dealer knows a forgery when he sees one. So does Hugh Pentecost's artist-and-sometime-sleuth, **John Jericho**, who debuted in 1967's *Dead Woman of the Year*.

Partners in Crime

She was the fifth daughter of Arch Deacon Cowley; he was a wounded hero from World War I. They had been childhood friends who met years later and decided to become *partners in crime* when they formed "Young Adventurers Ltd." in London. They are, of course, Agatha Christie's bon vivant duo, **Prudence Cowley** and **Tommy Beresford**. With their combined ages not even totaling forty-five, **Tommy** and **Tuppence** burst on the scene in 1922's *The Secret Adversary* as two young adventurers-for-hire who'll do most anything for money. "Most anything" often turns out to be solving crimes. The entertaining pair later marry and run sort of a detective agency.

Mignon G. Eberhart teamed a middle-aged spinster nurse named **Sarah Keate** with a young police detective named **Lance O'Leary** in the midwest of the 1930s. Sarah possessed an inquisitive nature and easily finds herself in peril with O'Leary, her rescuer. However, Nurse Keate does go on to solve two cases all on her own.

He was a retired private detective anxious to help his heiress wife spend her fortune while he swilled martinis and spent time walking his schnauzer, Asta. *The Thin Man* (1934) proved to be their only mystery case together, yet Dashiell Hammett's **Nick** and **Nora Charles** was such a popular couple that their adventures were extended by movies and television. Even today, mystery reviewers compare crime-solving duos to the happily married Nick and Nora.

Publisher **Jerry North** and his socialite wife **Pamela** also proved to be a big hit with readers. The husband and wife writing team of Richard and Frances Lockridge put their married amateurs in harm's way in over twenty-five novels as well as on radio and TV, beginning with the novel *The Norths Meet Murder* in 1940. The stories were rich with humor even though Pamela proved to be the perfect "had I but known" heroine—always in need of rescuing in the final chapter.

Despite the fact they solved eight murders together, **Colonel John Primrose** was quite formal when he talked with **Grace Latham**. The fifty-something West Point graduate and World War II hero mustered courage to ask the forty-something widow to be his wife after twelve adventures. Grace declined despite the fact that the Colonel always turned up in time to save her. But Leslie Ford's (1937) duo from Washington, DC's elegant Georgetown finally tie the knot after their fifteenth murder case that began with *By the Watchman's Clock.*

Henry and **Emily Bryce** find time to solve murders while they refinish furniture for decorators in downtown Manhattan in Margaret Scherf's 1949 mystery novel, *The Gun in Daniel Webster's Bust.* Aaron Marc Stein was also busy in 1949 creating American archaeologists, **Tim Mulligan** and **Elsie Mae Hunt**, who find bodies—and not of the ancient kind—on their digs as in *Days of Misfortune.*

Mirror Image

Peter Death Bredon Wimsey—Lord Peter—arguably the most famous amateur sleuth of all time created by Dorothy L. Sayers in 1923. The monocled aristocrat was almost too good to be true. Witty and urbane, Lord Peter was extremely intelligent, an expert sportsman, decorated war hero, accomplished pianist, rare book collector and noted student of criminology. He soon became London's leading amateur detective. Looked after by his former sergeant, Bunter, he's off "wherever my whimsy takes me" which, quite often, has him risking his life while solving complex whodunits.

Sayers introduced Wimsey in *Whose Body?* in 1923. In *Strong Poison*, **Harriet Vane**, on trial for murder, becomes Lord Peter's cause. He finds the real killer and then sets about wooing the fair Harriet. She keeps him at length, but not too far, when another murder case intrudes on their lives. Finally, in *Gaudy Night* (Sayers' twelfth Wimsey mystery), they realize they are

Author Eleanor Hyde says: "My favorite all-time amateur is Harriet Vane, who's feisty, witty and bright and has Lord Peter crazy for her. There have been quite a few take-offs on Harriet but so far no serious contenders."

truly suited to become more than just partners in solving crimes.

The responses we had from two hundred mystery writers, readers and librarians made Lord Peter Wimsey their favorite amateur detective. His believable personality traits were often viewed as his most endearing feature, as was the fact that the course of their true love hardly ran smooth!

Author Sally Gunning says: "I suppose my favorite sleuth has to be Lord Peter Wimsey. He's so debonair, so endearing."

America's Lord Peter would have to be S.S. VanDine's urbane **Philo Vance**. Vance seemed totally comfortable with his affected and Wimsey-like mannerisms and speech. Harvard educated, he, too, was of exceptional intelligence, interested in psychology, music, religion and art, and was eager to test his own theories on the human psyche. Vance used his interest in criminology to help his best friend, New York City's DA Markham, solve twelve baffling crimes; the first was 1926's *The Benson Murder Case*.

Bank on Them

Money, power and greed. Twist those traits together and they spell murder. In 1929, C.H.B. Kitchin had his young stockbroker, **Malcolm Warren**, play amateur detective in *Death of My Aunt* after he becomes a suspect when his rich aunt is murdered.

If you have your money in the Sloan Guaranty Trust Company, you can be sure it's very safe because of Senior Vice President **John Putnam Thatcher**. Emma Lathen created the sixty-something urbane Thatcher in 1961's *Banking* *on Death*. In more than fifteen outings, Thatcher's expertise in the financial world is called into play to solve extremely topical plots.

"Class, Take Out Pen and Paper and Take Notes . . ."

No one was at all surprised when teachers began appearing as amateur detectives. They certainly had personal knowledge of the nature of countless students, dogged determination to make sure all questions and problems were answered and solved perfectly, and their superior intellect was a given. Enter **Hildegarde Withers**. Replete with an extensive wardrobe of odd hats, Hildy was never at a loss to find clues or suspects when it came to helping her friend Inspector Oscar Piper of the NYPD. Stuart Palmer's horsey descriptions of Hildegarde were hardly flattering but she knew how to solve *The Penguin Pool Murder* in 1931 and seven other cases.

Leonidas Witherall (1938) looked like the famous Bard, William Shakespeare, which was why his students and friends called him Bill. As headmaster at a New England prep school, Witherall had time to write thriller novels and solve crimes penned by Phoebe Atwood Taylor writing as Alice Tilton.

Edmund Crispin's **Gervase Fen** was a professor of English and literature at Oxford when he wasn't solving crimes or writing literary critiques in eight novels that began with *The Case of the Gilded Fly* in 1944.

The Camera Never Lies

He was a hard-drinking tough guy with a hair-trigger temper and a deep hatred of criminals. **Jack "Flashgun" Casey** took photos for the Boston Express in 1934. George H. Coxe's amateur was able to combine his photo scoops with solving some of Boston's most heinous crimes as in *Silent Are the Dead*.

Coxe wasn't content with having one ace photographer on the scene. A year later, he created **Kent Murdock**, picture chief of the *Boston Courier Herald*. Murdock's crime scene photos were often stolen because they always proved to be the answer to "whodunit." Murdock's debut novel was *The Charred Witness*.

Busy novelist Craig Rice, also known as Georgiana Randolph, sent her two sidewalk photographers and con men, **Bingo Riggs** and **Handsome Kusak**, to a turkey farm in Iowa in 1943 to solve *The Thursday Turkey Murders*.

Filing a Claim?

Jefferson DiMarco should be everyone's insurance adjuster. Doris Miles Disney's honest man at Boston's Commonwealth Insurance often becomes too emotionally involved with his clients. In his first outing in *Dark Road* (1946), DiMarco falls in love with a woman who has killed one of his company's policyholders.

MacDonald Hastings' **Montague Cork** (1951) is the general manager of the Anchor Insurance Company. The elderly Cork can spot a false claim without blinking an eye.

Doris Miles Disney added U.S. Postal Inspector **David Madden** to her list of accomplished amateurs. Her highly researched series of three mystery novels featuring Madden began with *Unappointed Rounds* in 1956.

Unforgettable

Ask most women mystery writers, librarians and fans who was the first amateur detective they ever read and **Nancy Drew** is the name most spoken. (Some of us even made sure our purses contained everything Nancy had in her purse and that information was gleaned from reading all her adventures!) Nancy was intelligent, brave, beautiful, loved by everyone and knew how to get clues that solved the cases that baffled her lawyer father, Carson Drew.

Nancy Drew was the second most favorite of all amateur detectives. Her legions of fans are still growing today as many authors have become Carolyn Keene in the updated *Nancy Drew Files*. Edward Stratemeyer, and later his daughter Harriet Adams, created a young adult mystery dynasty—over eighty million copies sold—with Nancy Drew as well as **Joe** and **Frank Hardy** of **The Hardy Boys** fame.

From her first appearance in 1930, when she jumped into her roadster and solved the *Secret of the Old Clock*, Nancy Drew managed to form a seemingly ageless bond with every girl who ever read one of her adventures.

Many fans noted that Nancy Drew should be christened the "mother of the modern female PI." Why? Because Nancy certainly exhibited all of their modern traits: she was all business during a case; nothing deterred her from pursuing every clue and following a suspect (one person pointed out that Nancy had been knocked unconscious over one hundred times and always got up); and she was tough but vulnerable, and didn't need to have some guy rescue her in the last chapter (okay, so Ned Nickerson helped on occasion). Nancy Drew has stood tall and proud for over sixty-six years as a true amateur girl detective.

Over and over fans wrote of Nancy Drew: "She set us free from the image of the squeamish, male-dependent woman, who had to be handled gently. The woman sleuth who said: 'I'll have to ask permission to see if I can' and the 'Oh help, yeek!' Forever—we hope."

More than likely, we've missed a few "golden" amateur detectives but there are numerous compilations available as references. What should be apparent to you is the variety of amateur sleuths and how they reflected the society and history of their day. Notice, too, how the amateur's adeptness at solving baffling crimes, and their great intellect and clever insights all mirrored the knowledge of their authors. These great authors of amateur detective fiction created characters that were so remarkable, so memorable and so unique that they are still being read and enjoyed by readers today.

Next we'll take a look at why the amateur detective novel is still viable and popular today, as well as who's making up the current crop of amateur detectives, with comments from their authors.

CONTEMPORARY AMATEUR DETECTIVES

Law Enforcement and Technology

As a writer of amateur detective novels, you need to know how the criminal justice system has evolved and what, if any, difference that will make when you write your mystery. The most visible change in law enforcement lies in the technological advances that have occurred.

Technology has changed the face of law enforcement and crime detection. In the three hundred plus crime labs in the United States, over six hundred technicians and agents mix their street savvy ways with cutting-edge technology that includes computerized video, lasers and DNA analysis.

Computerized digital processing, or video enhancement, helps remove the blurriness and heighten the contrast on video-tape from surveillance cameras. Another computer process called microtopography makes it possible to create a three-dimensional digital map of the surface of a bullet. Laser beams can bring up the details of fingerprints that are a decade or more old plus restore altered prints for identification. DNA, the human genetic blueprint, can link body fluids to a specific person, making it a biochemical fingerprint. Add to these: enhanced procedures in developing hair, fiber and trace element evidence; handwriting comparisons; computerized evidence scanning; the FBI's National Crime Information Center's (NCIC) enormous computer network; and more highly developed forensic technology.

It's quite obvious that even a twentieth-century Dr. Thorndyke would have trouble competing with police technology without having access to a duplicate laboratory and equipment. Any sane person would ask, "Why in the world is the amateur detective still around, let alone thriving?"

The Human Factor

The amateur detective novel still thrives because, while technology is an important part of criminal investigation, quite often the human factor negates technical evidence. The number of police officials who have been indicted on various crimes has risen sharply despite the fact that the overall crime rate has gone down. While law enforcement officials look better on TV and in the movies than the old Keystone Kops, the questionable conduct of police officers and federal agents has become front page news in various cities around the country.

Philadelphia, Pennsylvania, saw six officers of the 39th District Police Department plead guilty to charges of robbery, theft of federal funds, civil rights violations, obstruction of justice and the use of tainted or false evidence to gain over 1,400 convictions.

In the "Trial of the Century"—the State of California versus O.J. Simpson—courtesy of televised coverage, the world saw the main focus shift from the murders of Nicole Brown Simpson and Ronald Goldman to the Los Angeles Police Department. As the trial unfolded, the following facts were admitted by the LAPD: Police stated that they lost 1.5cc's of the 8cc's of blood they collected from the defendant; evidence collected from the house's back gate and the defendant's infamous Ford Bronco were contaminated, thus tainting the DNA results; photos of shoe prints at the crime scene were taken more than two weeks after the barriers had been removed; courtesy of the LAPD's own videotape, two of the responding officers were seen trampling over the murder scene and contaminating evidence; and, certainly not least, was lead Detective Mark Fuhrman's admitted racism and statements of planting evidence in other cases.

The FBI's own crime lab was cited for sloppiness, misconduct and offering misleading or fabricated evidence to help the government's case in a number of high-profile criminal trials. It didn't help when Congress began investigating both the Bureau of Alcohol, Tobacco and Firearms (ATF) for the Ruby Ridge/White Supremacist debacle, and the FBI for its controversial handling of the showdown in Waco with fanatical religious leader David Koresh. And around the country, various groups like *Parents Against Corruption & Coverup* have surfaced because police sloppiness has failed to provide justice.

The majority of police officers are not bad; they are human beings trying to do a job. Most departments admit they are overworked and don't have the time or resources to pursue all the angles of a case. They tend to focus only on a particular suspect. So family and friends, of either the victim or suspect, look to someone else to find the real culprit, and it doesn't have to be a private detective.

Enter the Amateur Sleuth

Today's amateurs are equally as clever, inventive and resourceful as their earlier counterparts. With or without police cooperation or crime lab information and with a thumbed nose at the U.S. Constitution, the amateur can conduct searches without warrants, entrap at their leisure and use all of the technology that is publicly and privately available to ferret out who really did it.

Yes, the amateur may encounter certain problems like being arrested for breaking and entering, trespassing, obstruction of justice or aiding and abetting, and they certainly don't want to

"Why amateur sleuths? Because without all the technical information, an amateur (and his/her author) must focus on character, which is my favorite part of the book." Author Barbara Burnett Smith

be on the wrong end of the culprit's gun. Most notably, however, today's amateur sleuths are heralded for their intuition, powers of observation and deduction, and intellect along with their strong personalities.

Today's mystery writers have done their golden-age counterparts one better in creativity by exploring various ethnic and lifestyle cultures, expanding the historical role of the amateur and mixing in other genre themes of romance and science fiction. Once again, amateur sleuths are appearing in the most unusual places, some with unique professions and equally unique associates.

Today's Top Amateur Sleuths

Carolyn G. Hart is most often mentioned by the more than two hundred respondents to our poll as the American successor to Agatha Christie. Her best-known amateur sleuth is **Annie Laurance Darling** (along with professional problem-solver-for-hire husband, Max, and her eccentric mother-in-law Laurel), who owns the fabulous Death on Demand Bookstore in South Carolina. Fans love Annie because she is "lively, witty and imaginative with an ingrained sense of moral justice—all the ingredients of a top-notch sleuth." Carolyn generously gives many of today's current mystery authors extra publicity by having Annie

From author Carolyn G. Hart: "Sometimes I'm asked, 'Why do you want to write about murder?' I always know immediately that I am not talking to a mystery reader, because murder is never the point of a mystery. The focus is fractured relationships."

> Margaret Maron, says: "Even my professional sleuth, Sigrid Harald, may be a police officer but functions very much like amateurs in that they rely less upon technical hardware than on a basic understanding of the human heart under stress."

shelve and sell their novels. *Death on Demand* started the series that has won Agatha, Anthony and Macavity awards.

Margaret Maron's heralded amateur is **Judge Deborah Knott** of North Carolina. Margaret is examining contemporary North Carolina and the conflicts that arise as the state moves from a rural agrarian culture into a more high-tech urbanized society. In 1992, she swept all the mystery awards (Agatha, Anthony, Edgar and Macavity) for Deborah's first series book, *Bootlegger's Daughter*. Fans note that Deborah (and Margaret) have restored the moral fable aspect to the amateur sleuth.

Jenny Cain, director of Port Frederick, Massachusetts' charitable foundation, is Nancy Pickard's multi-award winning amateur sleuth. Jenny first appeared in 1984's *Generous Death* and acquired husband, Geoff, in 1987 in *Marriage Is Murder*.

Whether you call her Elizabeth Peters or Barbara Michaels, the talented Barbara Mertz writes mysteries to die for. Her intrepid, witty and incisive sleuth is Victorian feminist and archaeologist **Amelia Peabody**. Amelia, along with husband Radcliffe and precocious son Ramses, deals with villains who try to plunder Egyptian treasures. *Crocodile on the Sandbank* introduced Amelia to Radcliff and to their adoring fans in 1975.

The Best Occupations for Amateur Sleuths

In the hands of today's talented mystery writers, almost any profession or even lack of, due to unemployment or retirement, can

> Author Katherine Hall Page says: "My favorites are Christie, Sayers, Marsh, Virginia Rich and Nancy Pickard. What they have in common, besides mostly amateur sleuths, is a sense of humor and a good puzzle."

From author Sara Hoskinson Frommer: "As for amateurs, I like down-to-earth sorts such as Dorothy Cannell's Ellie and Elizabeth Daniels Squires' Peaches. Amelia Peabody and Ramses have no equals."

turn an everyday Jane or Joe into an amateur detective. *Nearly 90 percent of amateur detective novels are character driven,* meaning the reading public is more interested in becoming one with the character and enjoying his or her sleuthing talents and smarts rather than wading through pages of writing that detail autopsy results, DNA lab information or tedious procedural protocols. (There is certainly a large market for police procedural novels, but that's not what we're concerned with here.)

The reader is also willing to suspend disbelief when it comes to the amateur sleuth novel. Let's face it—just how many murders do everyday people become involved in and solve, especially on a continuing basis? Finishing up twelve years as TV's reigning mystery writer/amateur sleuth, Jessica Fletcher, of "Murder, She Wrote" fame, discovered enough dead bodies to christen herself the "Typhoid Mary" of tiny Cabot Cove, Maine. The joke is: Never invite Jessica Fletcher to visit because someone will die!

As a writer of amateur detective fiction, you should know that there are some professions that allow an amateur a wider arena in which to sleuth, and a slightly more logical premise by which they encounter all those corpses.

Law

"Lawyers enjoy a little mystery, you know." So said Sir Impey Biggs in Dorothy L. Sayers' *Clouds of Witness.* And right he (and she) was. Today's crop of lawyers and judges who go that extra step for their client and become the detectives that solve the case include: Margaret Millar's **Tom Aragon** and Julie Smith's defense attorney, **Rebecca Schwartz.** Paul Levine has turned former linebacker **Jake Lassiter** into a witty but cynical lawyer in *Slashback.*

English barristers include Frances Fyfield's London Crown

Prosecutor **Helen West**. When you need a medieval law professor head for Oxford's **Hilary Tamar** written by Sarah Caudwell. For scandal, politics and intrigue in the Anglican church, read Kate Charles' artist and solicitor pair **Lucy Kingsley** and **D. Middleton-Brown** in *A Dead Man out of Mind*.

Writing and Journalism

While writing is normally a solitary occupation, today's authors and journalists are seldom alone when they leave their creative endeavors to seek clues and the truth. Check out M.K. Loren's Shakespearean professor cum mystery writer, **Winston Marlowe Sherman**. Romance novelist's turned amateur sleuth include: Susan Rogers Cooper's **E.J. Pugh** and Elizabeth Peters' **Jacqueline Kirby**. Freelancing becomes deadly when Lora Roberts' **Liz Sullivan** looks around her neighborhood, and running a fashion magazine can be dangerous if you're Eleanor Hyde's **Lydia Miller**.

Whether they're writing for magazines, newspapers or TV, or taking photos, these investigative reporters are tenacious when it comes to tracing a story (or a clue). They will literally go to the ends of the earth to get the truth and the villain. When in blustery Chicago, look up Barbara D'Amato's **Cat Marsala**; Jan Burke's **Irene Kelly**; Pulitzer Prize-winning writer, Edna Buchanan's **Britt Montero** finds more than murder in Miami; and Gregory McDonald's **Irwin M. Fletcher** becomes a different man every hour when he's on a case.

Molly Cates is busy in award-winning author Mary Willis Walker's novels, as is Sarah Shankman's **Samantha Adams**. Mary Daheim's **Emma Lord** edits a small town newspaper while Lillian Jackson Braun's **Jim Qwilleran** gets expert sleuthing help from cats **Koko** and **Yum Yum** in her best-selling series.

In England, Hazel Holt's **Sheila Malory** leads an ordinary life (except for running into murders) as she writes for a British literary magazine; Audrey Peterson's **Jane Winfield** mixes journalism with music writing; and in Toronto, Alison Gordon's baseball newswriter is **Kate Henry**. John Feinstein has burned-out reporter **Bobby Kelleher** resting in New York but finding murder, while Betty Rowlands' British crime novelist **Melissa Craig** moves from London to a tiny cottage in Cotswold.

> One fan noted about Melissa Craig: " . . .She makes a delightful sleuth, without being cutesy or making cocktail party chatter about what is, after all, death."

Sometimes the camera lens gives the journalist an extra edge in seeing the truth of a situation. In New York, you'll find Shannon O'Cork's sports photographer, **Theresa Tracy Baldwin**, and in Calgary, you'll find Suzanne North's **Phoebe Fairfax** shouldering the video camera.

Edgar-winning author Wendy Hornsby tangles investigative filmmaker **Maggie MacGowen** in a complex crime that was inspired by the unsolved cases of LAPD Officer Mike Edwards. (Researching unsolved police cases might provide interesting ideas for writers of amateur detective fiction.)

England's famous television journalist, **Jemima Shore**, finds herself in and out of trouble from the busy pen of equally daring author Lady Antonia Fraser. Polly Whitney gained national recognition for her two broadcast journalists, **Abby Abagnarro**, director of TV's "Morning Watch," and his ex-wife and producer **Ike**. William L. DeAndrea's **Matt Cobb** sees a lot of action as VP in charge of special projects at a New York City TV network.

Medicine

Medical experts are driven by knowledge, nerve and rampant curiosity. These erstwhile doctors and nurses x-ray, prod and poke, not at their beloved patients, but at the truth of who committed the crime and why. Even the dead have tales to tell Chief Medical Examiner **Kay Scarpetta** in the best-selling series by Patricia Cornwell, and in mysteries featuring Louise Hendrickson's crime lab physician **Amy Prescott** as well as Aaron Elkins' forensic anthropologist **Gideon Oliver**.

Carolyn Chambers Clark writes about registered nurse **Megan Baldwin** as does Mary Kittredge, who pens **Edwina Crusoe**'s adventures.

You can rest easy when these doctors are on staff: E.X. Ferrars' physiotherapist **Virginia Freer** and Jonathan

Kellerman's psychologist **Dr. Alex Delaware**.

There's even danger ahead for veterinarians, and not just from animals. Laura Crum's horse vet, **Gail McCarthy**, and Lydia Adamson's rural vet, **Deidre Quinn Nightingale**, have solved their share of mysteries as have Barbara Block's pet store owner, **Robin Light**, and Carolyn Bank's equestrienne sleuth, **Robin Vaughn**.

Teaching

Teachers and professors are still ruling more than students. Luckily, with all the high school and college reunions, the visiting academics who bring trouble in their briefcases, and the lecture circuits to hit, teachers and professors won't soon run out of crimes to solve.

Award-winning author Bill Crider once remarked that he may have made his college campus a bit too small for all the dead bodies that kept appearing.

Hamilton Crane's retired British art teacher and extraordinary amateur sleuth is the indomitable **Emily D. Seeton** who could share one-to-one adventures with Amanda Cross' **Kate Fansler**. Sharyn McCrumb writes about two award-winning academic sleuths in anthropologist **Elizabeth MacPherson** and college professor **James Owen Mega**, who writes science fiction. Charlotte MacLeod keeps botany professor **Peter Shandy** and his librarian wife, **Helen Marsh Shandy**, busy with murder in rural Maine.

In Texas, look for Bill Crider's **Carl Burns**; at Philly prep, Gillian Roberts' high school teacher **Amanda Pepper**; and Teri Holbrook's southern historian **Gale Grayson**.

P.M. Carlson's statistician and mom, **Maggie Ryan**, keeps busy in late 1960s New York City.

Antique and Art Collecting

Hunting for antiques or acquiring objets d'art for museums can be a highly adventurous career that is downright deadly at times. Risking life and limb so that we can all gaze in wonder at paintings and sculpture are: Clarissa Watson's **Persis Willum**; Elizabeth Peters' **Vicky Bliss**; and John Malcom's art investor in London, **Tim Simpson**. Jake Page has blind sculptor **Mo Bowdre** and his Hopi girlfriend, **Connie Barnes**, solving crimes in the art world.

Sometimes agents give their respective clients a bit more than just good contract negotiations. Tierney McClellan's real estate agent, **Schuyler Ridgway** of Louisville, has to explain why she was left a small fortune by a murder victim she never met. Charlaine Harris' **Aurora "Roe" Teagarden** becomes a real estate agent and finds a corpse in a house she's showing. Harlan Coben's sports agent, **Myron Bolitar**, has to deal with more than his baseball client.

Business and Finance

When you step into the world of business and high finance, you cross the line into an arena teeming with greed, power and lust. Corporate intrigue abounds, as does money laundering, double sets of books and product espionage. These engaging amateur sleuths not only do their jobs but manage to solve the most heinous and complex crimes as well.

Check out Annette Meyers' Wall Street headhunters **Xenia Smith** and **Leslie Wetzon**. Ask for investment advice from A.E. Maxwell's **Fiddler** and **Fiora Flynn** or Dianne G. Pugh's **Iris Thorne**. Need a good CPA? Try Connie Feddersen's **Amanda Hazard** or J. Dayne Lamb's **Teal Stewart**.

Computer Programming

If you suspect computer fraud, give L.A. Taylor's expert **J.J. Jamison**, Carolyn A. Haddad's **Becky Belski**, or Susan Holtzer's **Anneka Haagen** a chance at restoring missing files. Susan says that Anneka is a woman of a certain age who is drawn into detecting and a relationship rather against her will.

If you're in England and need computer help, try calling Susan B. Kelly's software designer **Alison Hope**, who can also call on Detective Inspector **Nick Trevellyan** for assistance. Computer programmer **Laura Fleming** of Boston finds mysteries to solve whenever she goes home to Byerly, North Carolina, in Toni L.P. Kelner's series.

Author Susan Holtzer speaks for a lot of fans: "I'm particularly fond of those amateurs who are written with a certain seriousness, and who deal with real issues in real life."

Public Relations

Want to increase business but downplay that dead body in the front office? Try Carol Brennan's PR consultant **Liz Wareham**, or Carole Nelson Douglas' **Temple Barr** and her cat in their series debut 1992's *Catnap*.

Small Business Ownership

Even running a small business can be life threatening—just ask Jaqueline Girdner's **Kate Jasper**. Kate is a vegetarian, practices tai chi and lives in Mill Valley, California, where she owns and runs Jest Gifts, a novelty company.

Then there's Sally Gunning's **Peter Bartholomew**. Peter owns an odd-job company called Factotum on Nashtoba Island (Cape Cod?), which allows him to do anything and find bodies. Sally reiterates Bill Crider's concern about the body count piling up on Nashtoba when the population is only 800.

Culinary Arts

Candlelight, crystal, china, delicious gourmet cuisine and a stunning ice sculpture—no, wait, that's the host in a block of ice and he hasn't paid his bill! Caterers, food critics, chefs and restaurateurs have become some of the most creative amateur sleuths in recent years. If you like murder on the menu, try inviting these culinary artists to your next affair: Janet Laurence's **Darina Lisle**; Nan and Ivon Lyons' pair, **Natasha O'Brien** and **Millie Ogden**; and Amy Myers'

Author Sally Gunning echoes other writers of amateur sleuth novels when she says: "The thing I like best is that amateurs have lives outside the confines of the murder mystery, and the mystery is often an offshoot of something else going on in their lives that's at least equally interesting."

Auguste Didier. Don't forget Diane Mott Davidson's Colorado caterer **Goldy Bear Schulz** and the mouthwatering recipes that delight fans.

Katherine Hall Page's **Faith Sibley Fairchild** was a caterer in Manhattan who relocated to the tiny village of Aleford, Massachusetts, after marrying the Rev. Thomas Fairchild. You can sample the food at **Jane Lawless**' restaurant; she and reviewer **Sophie Greenway** solve crimes courtesy of their author Ellen Hart. Nancy Pickard is finishing the late Virginia Rich's **Eugenia Potter** series and Camilla Crespi's fabulously funny Italian transplant **Simona Griffo** can provide you with more than recipes to sink your teeth into.

Camilla likens Simona's logic to the best Gruyere—lots of holes. But she does get to the truth by sheer doggedness, much to the concern of her lover, homicide detective Stan Greenhouse.

Camilla Crespi says: "What most attracted me to mystery series was their reliability. You open up Miss Marple and she hasn't changed on you. Same habits, same quirks, same friends. . . and you know she'll solve the problem in the end."

If you want to spice things up, try adding a dash of herbs from **China Bayles**' garden and the pen of Susan Wittig Albert. Claudia Bishop's chef and inn owner sisters, **Sarah** and **Meg Quilliam**, can offer you a place to sleep, even if it's fitful, as can Mary Daheim's **Judith McMonigle**, Tamar Myers' Mennonite inn owner, **Magdalena Yoder**, and Jean Hager's **Tess Darcy**, who runs the Iris House bed and breakfast inn.

Library Science and Bookstore Ownership

Libraries and bookstores seem to attract an often entertaining regular clientele as well as criminals, overdue books and shoplifters. Check out librarian **Helma Zukas** in Jo Dereske's "Miss Zukas and" series, Kate Morgan's senior **Dewey James** and Sheila Simonson's **Lark Dailey Dodge**.

If you want to buy books, Joan Hess' sassy Arkansas native **Claire Malloy** can make you die laughing while you're hunting for something to read. M.K. Wren's former intelligence agent, **Conan Flagg**, is half Irish, half Nez Perce and sleuths in the tradition of Ellery Queen with a little John D. MacDonald thrown in.

Environmentalism

Ahh, wilderness and the great outdoors, birds twittering, fabulous sunsets and a corpse. Environmentalists and their tactics have sparked political and economic debates that have exploded on the front pages of many newspapers. It was only a matter of time until writers started creating amateur sleuths to handle investigating crimes in this arena. Way up north in Alaska you'll find Sue Henry's sled dog racer, **Jessie Arnold**, running in the Iditarod just ahead of a killer. Elizabeth Quinn's wildlife investigator, **Lauren Maxwell**, is also patrolling the Yukon. Award-winning author Nevada Barr's park ranger, **Anna Pigeon**, keeps her eyes open as does Lee Wallingford's forest fire dispatcher, **Ginny Trask**.

Farther afield, you'll find American safari guide **Jazz Jasper** asking questions in Kenya in the series created by Karin McQuillan; in London, Ann Cleeves' bird-watcher **Molly Palmer-Jones** has husband **George** sharing sleuthing duties.

Susan Dunlap's meter reader, **Vejay Haskell**, is busy searching for clues as is Sarah Andrews' oil worker, **Em Hansen**. Author Andrews puts Em in the position of having to solve a geological puzzle in order to solve a murder. Ruth Raby Moen's **Kathleen O'Shaughnessy** stumbles on illegally dumped nuclear waste in the state of Washington.

Show Business

Backstabbing, blackmail, payola—welcome to the entertainment business, fertile ground for any writer or amateur sleuth. Some actor or actress is always dying, either in reviews or on stage, and the behind-the-scenes skullduggery is infamous. In New York, try to get an interview with: Dorian Yeager's actor, writer and playwright, **Victoria Bowering**; Jane Detinger's Broadway actress and director, **Jocelyn O'Roarke**; Dorothy Salisbury Davis' actress cum columnist, **Julie Hayes**; Lydia Adamson's actress and cat lover, **Alice Nestleton**; Simon Brett's over-the-hill actor, **Charles Paris**; and Stefanie Matteson's Oscar-winning actress, **Charlotte Graham**.

Charlotte Graham, now in her seventies, is a veteran of Hollywood's golden age. She's been married four times and has had several notorious affairs.

Author Stefanie Matteson speaks to amateur sleuths and credibility: "The fact that Charlotte is so famous has helped make her a more believable amateur sleuth, who by their very natures tend to strain the reader's credibility. Her fame gives her a natural authority . . . people are naturally eager to talk to her. And her many connections help her solve the crime."

In Hollywood, look up Marlys Millhiser's literary agent, **Charlie Green**; in Seattle, look up lounge singer, **Jane da Silva**, from K.K. Beck; and in London, you'll find Marian Babson's aging movie queens, **Eve Sinclair** and **Trixie Dolan**.

One fan noted of Jane da Silva: "She's an outstanding character. She seems like an actual person, expressing astonishment, disbelief, tolerance, curiosity and feckless determination. She copes with danger and physical emergency without superhuman powers."

Senior Sleuthing

Forty used to be fatal, then it was bumped to fifty, then sixty. As the baby boomers grow older, making a specific age equal senility has gone out of fashion. Even though Miss Jane Marple might be their hero, you'll very rarely find any of these senior sleuths in rocking chairs or gumming their Jell-O. They are sharp, tenacious and resourceful when it comes to helping family and friends who are in need of a detective.

Dorothy Gillman created the grandmotherly CIA agent, **Mrs. Pollifax**, in 1966 and her adventures have been amazing readers since. D.B. Borton has her sixty-something **Cat Caliban** working as a PI in training, while Elizabeth Daniels Squire has her over-fifty, absentminded sleuth, **Peaches Dann**,

Social worker Joan Robbins, who teaches a course on women and detective fiction, says: "What is special about (senior) novels is their portrayal of women as vital, energetic, thoughtful, curious risk takers . . . and other characteristics which enable us to move away from stereotypical views of older people."

using memory tricks to help her solve crimes.

Corrine Holt Sawyer created two seventy-plus admirals' widows named **Angela Benbow** and **Caledonia Wingate**, who act as deputies for their luxury retirement home. You couldn't find two more opposite seniors than the late Mary Bowen Hall's salvage dealer, **Emma Chizzit**, and Irene Allen's Quaker widow, **Elizabeth Elliot**.

American widow, sixtyish **Dorothy Martin**, recently moved to the cathedral town of Sherebury, England, where she stumbled over the body of a dead clergyman in Jeanne M. Dams' mystery series.

Meet **Fanny Zindel**, a decidedly curious Jewish grandmother who's been asked to join the Israeli Mossad in Serita Stevens' series. Then there's Sherry Lewis' **Fred Vickery**, a stalwart seventy-two-year-old who lives in a small town in the Colorado Rockies. He's retired from being a buildings and grounds super for the local school district, and his involvement with crime comes from his deep concern for his neighbors and family (a trait common to all amateur sleuths).

Margot Arnold's sprightly senior duo of American anthropologist **Penny Spring** and British archaeologist **Sir Toby Glenower** circle the globe for their profession and encounter murder.

The Occult

Bubble, bubble, toil and trouble—from ancient Roman soothsayers to Nostradamus, I Ching to voodoo practitioners—psychics are still viable detectives. Don't scoff. The United States government just admitted spending twenty million dollars on psychic intelligence gathering. And there have been numer-

An interesting comment from Stefanie Matteson, who writes of senior sleuth actress Charlotte Graham: "She is in her mid-seventies, which is getting up there. I have solved this problem in recent books by setting them back in time. But I don't know how I'm going to deal with this problem (age) in the future."

ous accounts of psychics helping police agencies around the world solve crimes and locate missing people. Try these occult practitioners: Rosemary Edghill's graphic designer, **Karen Hightower**, is also a practicing white witch; Linda Mather's astrologer **Jo Hughes**; Mignon Warner's British clairvoyant, **Edwina Charles**; and Nancy Atherton's frumpy **Emma Porter** gets a ghostly guide in **Aunt Dimity**.

Martha C. Lawrence has psychotherapist **Elizabeth Chase** abandoning her practice to focus her psychic ability on solving crimes. Author Lawrence uses a believable blend of investigative techniques and psychic information to catch a killer.

Religious Vocations

Besides tending to their religious duties, these nuns, priests, deacons and laypeople make it their business to cleanse the souls of the damned while they bring them to justice for their crimes. William X. Kienzle keeps **Father Koesler** busy while Andrew M. Greeley has **Bishop Blackie Ryan** looking for killers.

Sister Carol Anne O'Marie pens mysteries featuring septuagenarian nun **Sister Mary Helen** and her cohort, **Sister Eileen**. In England, you'll find **Sister Joan** investigating the murder of the rectory housekeeper at the Convent of the Daughters of Compassion in Veronica Black's novel. Diane M. Greenwood has British deaconess **Rev. Theodora Braithwaite** looking for clerical errors as does Isabelle Holland's Episcopal priest, **Rev. Claire Aldington**. Carrie Brown's **Lindy Adair** is a "compassionate ride-along," which means she's a volunteer who accompanies police when they carry tragic news to families. She has a Ph.D. in comparative religion, a background that gives her the confidence she needs to approach strangers sympathetically.

Retro-Sleuthing

Amateur sleuths are not a contemporary phenomena, and some of the most inventive writing has brought us historical sleuths of heroic proportions. Some authors have integrated their fictional character into real historical situations and people. Arguably the most famous is the late Ellis Peters' award-winning **Brother Cadfael**. The good Brother is a twelfth-century Welshman at the Benedictine monastery of St. Peter and St. Paul in England where he also dabbles in herbs.

Candace Robb melds true events with fiction when her fourteenth-century Welshman **Owen Archer** solves a series of murders for the Archbishop of York. Margaret Frazer has her medieval nun, **Sister Frevisse**, who is a hosteler at St. Frideswide's priory. In twelfth-century France, ex-novice **Catherine Le Vendeur** finds a stolen relic and Christian-Jewish conflict in Sharan Newman's series. Even earlier, in seventh-century Ireland, Peter Tremayne has **Sister Fidelma** and **Brother Eadulf** involved in intrigue among the ancient Celts. Lynda S. Robinson deftly takes on ancient Egyptian political intrigue with **Lord Meren**, who is confidant and advisor to the boy-king Tutankhamen.

Sigismondo is the Italian agent of the Duke of Rocca. These Renaissance mysteries by Elizabeth Eyre are filled with the rich historical background of the times as well as all the intrigue and conspiracies. In seventeenth-, eighteenth- and nineteenth-century New York you'll find Maan Meyer's series based on the descendants of the first sheriff **Pieter Tonneman**.

The Victorian era has spawned Ann Crowleigh's delightful sisters, **Miranda** and **Clare Clively**; Robin Paige's **Kathryn Ardleigh**, an American author who gets called to England to aide her aunt; and Emily Brightwell's series featuring **Inspector Witherspoon** and his housekeeper **Mrs. Jeffries**. Anne Perry's Victorian sleuths **Charlotte** and **Thomas Pitt** have to determine if Jack the Ripper has returned.

Suffragette sleuths show up on both sides of the Atlantic fighting for women's causes and clues in the form of Gillian

Linscott's British **Nell Bray**, and Miriam Grace Monfredo's **Glynis Tryon** in Seneca Falls, New York.

In Paris, Carole Nelson Douglas has turned the only woman to outwit Sherlock Holmes, **Irene Adler**, into a sleuth. Douglas makes the position of women in Victorian society a key ingredient in the series.

Kate Kingsbury's Edwardian hotel owner, **Cecily Sinclair**, keeps things humming at the Pennyfoot Hotel; in Tudor England, Charlaine Harris has proprietress **Lily Bard** doing housecleaning and running errands; and Joan Smith has gone back to Regency England in creating **Dowager Countess de Coventry**.

Marian J.A. Jackson has **Abigail Patience Danforth** as a turn-of-the-century consulting detective in various locales and features real people who were actually there at the time, including Arthur Conan Doyle, Marshall Bill Tilghman, Jack London and Houdini.

Author Bruce Alexander brings to life the nineteenth-century legendary blind judge, **Sir John Fielding**, along with his Watson, thirteen-year-old Jeremy Proctor.

The Roaring Twenties has K.K. Beck's **Iris Cooper** becoming a coed at Stanford while on the other side of the world, **Phryne Fisher** is sleuthing in 1920s Australia courtesy of Kerry Greenwood. Carola Dunn brings 1923 into full view with the **Honourable Daisy Dalrymple**, daughter of a viscount who chooses to earn her own living rather than sponge off her widowed mother.

In nearer history, Elliott Roosevelt has his mother, **First Lady Eleanor**, investigating when a body is found after a state visit from the King and Queen of England.

Ethnic/Minority Sleuthing

Ethnic sleuths have made a strong appearance and developed an equally strong following in the past few years. Look for **C.F. Floyd**, a black bail bondsman in Denver, in Robert O. Greer's novel. Black author, Barbara Neely, created middle-aged black domestic **Blanche White** and immediately won the Agatha, Anthony and Macavity Awards.

One fan noted: "Blanche gets in a mess and works her way out of it with skill, humor and a lot of consciousness-raising comments about the toll of racism on both whites and blacks."

Native American sleuths have emerged as well. Jean Hager pens **Molly Bearpaw**, a Cherokee civil rights investigator in Oklahoma (as well as half-Cherokee **Police Chief Mitch Bushyhead**); Nina Romberg writes about Caddo-Commanche medicine woman, **Marian Winchester**, in Texas; and Chelsea Quinn Yarbro has a series featuring attorney and Ojibway tribal shaman, **Charles Spotted Moon**.

In Margaret Coel's *The Eagel Catcher*, she creates sleuth **Father John O'Malley**, a Jesuit priest and recovering alcoholic who's been exiled for the last six years to the St. Francis Mission on the Wind River Reservation in Wyoming. He partners with **Vicky Holden**, an Arapaho who ventured into the white world to become a lawyer and has now returned to the reservation to help her people.

J.F. Trainor has created a unique Native American Anishinabe princess in **Angela Biwaban**. To pay for her mother's cancer treatment, Angela embezzled funds from the tax assessor's office where she worked. While serving three years in a South Dakota correctional facility, she learned a variety of criminal skills. Since her release, Angela has put those skills to good use as a modern-day Lone Ranger, avenging family and friends who've been victimized by wealthy, politically protected crooks. The FBI has a warrant out for her, code name: Pocahontas.

There's been a positive mainstream response by readers to gay and lesbian amateur sleuths. Take time to investigate: Nikki Baker's lesbian stockbroker, **Virginia Kelly**; Val McDermid's lesbian journalist, **Lindsay Gordon**; Barbara Wilson's printing company owner, **Pam Nilsen**; and lesbian activist **Emma Victor** from Mary Wings. **Tyler Jones**, Joan Drury's lesbian, writes about women and violence.

Ellen Hart's **Jane Lawless** is gay and runs a restaurant in

Minneapolis. The latest book in the series, *A Small Sacrifice*, just won both the 1995 Lambda Literary Award and the Minnesota Book Award.

Author Ellen Hart says: "This book is probably my favorite. It's about friendship, a topic that's very important to me. And I felt extremely close to the characters in that book."

C.C. Scott is a semiretired therapist who, along with her lesbian partner, teacher **Barbara Bettencourt**, deals with murder and blackmail. Author Pele Plante notes that "mid-fifty is not all that old, but the stories include issues of aging and feature complex older characters."

Tony Fennelly writes of New Orleans scion, **Matt Sinclair**, who is pressed into service as a sleuth when police Lieutenant Frank Washington threatens to look into his relationship with his nineteen-year-old live-in lover, Robin.

In Minneapolis, a star TV journalist is outed when his gay lover is murdered in R.D. Zimmerman's *Closet: A Todd Mills Mystery*. In Boston, gay hairdresser **Stan Kraychick** is *Dead on Your Feet* in Grant Michaels' new novel.

Pauli Golden and her lover, **Chessie Anaya**, try to survive as a couple and manage a suburban fitness club in Carole Spearin McCauley's *A Winning Death*.

Motherly Sleuthing

Mom is still asking questions and she knows who is lying—no matter what their age or occupation. Suburban moms have turned sleuth in Chicago where Jill Churchill's single mom, **Jane Jeffry**, is busy with family and murder; in the Bay area, Jonnie Jacobs' single mom is **Kate Austen**; in New England you'll find Leslie Meier's **Lucy Stone** and Valerie Wolzien's **Susan Henshaw**.

In the small college town of Oliver, Indiana, **Joan Spencer** plays viola in the civic symphony and directs the Senior Citizen's Center, all while being mom to her teenage son Andrew. Author Sara Hoskinson Frommer says Joan doesn't set out to get involved in murder, it just seems to happen around her.

Author Carole McCauley says: "I'm glad there's room for this 'human interest' category (amateur sleuths) compared with forensic mystery heavy on technical detail, cop books, and private eye books that are only semibelievable. What I do is show that the average citizen can use the details of, and knowledge from, her work life to 'make a difference' to the crime wave."

Odd Jobs

Jacks- and Jills-of-all-trades still make wonderful amateur sleuths. By virtue of their various occupations, they come in contact with an ever-changing variety of situations that become logical extensions for their sleuthing talents. Liza Cody's **Eva Wylie** is a female wrestler, junkyard security guard and small-time criminal. Her first adventure, *Bucket Nut* (1993) won the British Silver Dagger mystery award. Jerome Doolittle has a wrestler sleuth and technological Robin Hood in his **Tom Bethany**. Linda Mariz turned University of Washington grad student and volleyball player, **Laura Ireland**, onto sleuthing. And on the golf pro circuit, Charlotte and Aaron Elkins bring young **Lee Ofsted** back to murders during a golf tournament.

Transplanted English author Dorothy Cannell is the creator of the award-winning **Ellie** and **Ben Haskell** series that also features the eccentric **Tramwell sisters**. Dorothy made quite a name for herself, as well as her overweight interior decorator Ellie and her aspiring chef husband in the first of the series, 1984's highly acclaimed *The Thin Woman*.

Another interior decorator who doubles as an amateur sleuth is Margaret Logan's **Olivia Chapman**, who made her debut in *The End of an Altruist*.

Tony Fennelly brings us **Margo Fortier**, a stripper turned society columnist after her marriage of convenience to a closeted gay aristocrat.

Although born in Texas, Patricia Highsmith lives in Switzerland and has created a charming Englishman forger in the person of **Tom Ripley**, who has been called "disturbing" because the character is a psychopath and impersonator.

If you want your house cleaned and a murder solved, call Atlanta and ask for **Callahan Garrity**, Kathy Hogan Trocheck's burned-out ex-cop.

Christine Andreae has created a cynical but compassionate amateur in the sharp-witted, wisecracking **Lee Squires**. Lee, who has no fixed address, house-sits to make ends meet and doubles as a camp cook in Montana in the summer.

Christine Andreae says: "I never thought of mysteries as inferior fiction. I grew up reading Nancy Drew."

Larry Block brings his award-winning writing talent to readers in novel after novel in the person of bookseller-by-day/burglar-by-night, **Bernie Rhodenbarr**.

Janet Evanovich created bail bondswoman **Stephanie Plum**; while best-selling author Nora Roberts, writing as J.D. Robb, went into the near future with her sleuth **Eve Dallas**.

Animals have become more than just a pet for today's amateur sleuths. Lillian Jackson Braun is the acknowledged originator of the feline focus in contemporary mystery novels with Koko and Yum Yum as previously noted. Author Rita Mae Brown, along with her cat Sneaky Pie, joined the mystery genre with postmistress **Mary Minor Haristeen** and her tiger cat **Mrs. Murphy**.

The canine contingency has Susan Conant's dog trainer, **Holly Winter**, and her malamute, **Rowdy**; Melissa Cleary has her college film instructor, **Jackie Walsh**, share sleuthing duties with **Jake**, a retired police dog that she adopted; and Laurien Berenson's **Melanie Travis** poses as a dog breeder to find her uncle's murderer.

As you can see, the listing of amateur sleuths could go on forever. We've certainly missed more than a few, but our goal was to give you an overview of today's sleuths and their professions. Authors have generously shared some of the problems they've encountered as well as some of the joys in writing about their amateur sleuths.

Next, we'll take a look at how you can make your amateur sleuth cultivate the talent and techniques that make this genre so popular.

T H R E E

RESUMÉ OF AN AMATEUR SLEUTH

More Than a Sharp Mind

When Edgar Allen Poe wrote, "Great intellects guess well," he was making a statement that not only applied to his sleuth Auguste Dupin but to all amateur detectives. "Golden age" mystery writers *told* the reader that their amateur detectives had sharp minds, a keen sense of observation, the ability to solve the most complicated riddles and puzzles, and an uncanny use of reason and logic—especially when it dealt with solving crimes.

In some of the earliest novels, the amateur's great intellect was supported by the fact that he had a larger than normal head—witness The Thinking Machine. Most of the time, however, the amateur sleuths were much like the Old Man in the Corner or Miss Jane Marple, seldom leaving the comfort of their rocking chairs to find the villain of the piece. They didn't need fingerprint experts or forensic lab reports. They were able to *listen* to the information at hand, *ask pertinent questions* that gave them more details and then, using logic and reasoning, *deduce the correct answer.*

But did they "just guess well"? Hardly. Amateurs of the past and present used more than guesswork to solve crimes. They all seemed to possess character traits that allowed them to obtain information or focus on details that the police dismissed.

The amateur sleuth has the advantage of not being bound by the rules that govern police or even private detectives. Legal issues such as Miranda Rights, search warrants and entrapment laws don't stop the amateur. They are free to use deception, guile, ruses—anything and everything to catch the criminal.

Yes, there are liabilities. The amateur sleuth who has invaded someone's home, office or car in their tireless search for clues, may be arrested for trespassing or breaking and entering. And, if their entrapment plan works, the amateur may have to worry about having some type of backup waiting just in case the situation gets out of control.

How to Create a Successful Amateur Sleuth

A writer's most important job is to create believable characters. Characters that are so real, so alive, so special that readers feel they can call them on the telephone or visit them in their homes or offices. In creating an amateur detective, a writer should focus on the characteristics that will make their sleuth believable—supermen and superwomen need not apply. A writer should use reality-based attributes seasoned with some highly developed traits that merge together and breathe life into their amateur sleuth's character.

One of the exciting things about being a writer is the ability to *become* your character. Previously, we mentioned how Poe and his sleuth, Dupin, were mirror images of each other. The character became the narrator of the author's senses, feelings, ideas and thoughts on a wide variety of topics. Today's authors are doing likewise by letting their amateur sleuths speak out on social issues, society's morals and the justice system.

Here are some traits that you can endow in your characters to make them credible and remarkable amateur sleuths.

Intuition. Sixth Sense. Hunch.

It's that little voice that tells your amateur sleuth that something is wrong, some person isn't being truthful or some piece of hard evidence is not what it appears to be. Women aren't the only ones who have intuition, although men prefer to call it a hunch.

Call it what you will, *intuition is the ability to know something is going to happen before it actually happens.* This doesn't mean that all amateur sleuths have psychic ability. What it does mean is that you are going to have to show your amateur sleuth listening to their inner voice.

When your sleuth gets into a new situation or meets new people, make your character react and pay attention to that immediate reaction. Your character needs to reference if his or her reaction was positive or negative. Are their senses heightened in awareness? Do sights, sounds and smells become stronger and cause a reaction? While snooping, do they feel prickles along their back that tell them they might not be as alone as they thought?

Had I but known, Mary Roberts Rinehart's much-maligned type of mystery story that has heroines endlessly getting into dangerous situations, isn't so off base. Apparently, her protagonists (along with countless other authors') didn't pay any attention to their intuition and constantly found themselves in need of being rescued.

Busybody. Gossip.

No truer words were ever spoken about the amateur detective. While the police are interested in "just the facts," the amateur doesn't mind listening to "that most knowing of persons—gossip" in an effort to gain some fascinating insights about both the suspect and victim.

"There is nothing so dangerous for anyone who has something to hide as conversation." Agatha Christie and her amateur sleuths knew that most people cannot resist revealing themselves and expressing their personalities through conversation.

Writer's Research Note

Statistics show that 90 percent of crime victims stated, after the fact, that they heard their inner voice warning them about a person or situation. Their rational mind, however, told them to be nice and ignore the warning and that they were being silly.

> —*Laine Jastram, executive director of Resources for Personal Empowerment, New York, NY, from the article "Five Ways to Conquer Your Fear" in the July 1995 issue of* McCall's.

The longer a person talks, the more opportunity they have to give themselves away.

The Ability to Get People to Talk

Your character needs to adopt a relaxed posture and nurturing manner. A disarming nature and soothing voice entices the other person to let their guard down and not feel threatened, which is easy since the amateur doesn't wear a uniform or flash a badge. Have your character bring out that pot of tea or coffee, maybe even a little nip, a scrumptious dessert or a box of recipes or old photographs. Anything to start and keep conversation (information) flowing.

Since you have created all the characters in your mystery novel, you know that you can't make it too easy for your sleuth. Create a reluctant witness that can show off your amateur's talent at ferreting out information. Try having them use the direct approach by saying: "I know this may be difficult, but how can we talk about it so that you'll be more comfortable?" Your amateur can take on hard-boiled traits with: "I would think *you'd* want to help find out what really happened." *Remember:* The amateur detective is tenacious and doesn't give up until they have their culprit.

Now you have to make your clever sleuth decide how much of the gossip is true and how much is a lie. If there's one thing we all know about the amateur, it's that they possess the innate ability to know the human personality, observe it and be able to separate truth from lies.

Truth or Lies?

Is it possible for an amateur sleuth to become a human lie detector? The Leakage Hypothesis states that a person's body naturally leaks clues when they are being deceitful. A lie detector works on this theory. Easy questions establishing a person's name, address and age form the base response that is then used for comparison when the more difficult questions are asked.

As a writer, you need to know what these leaked clues are to know if you want to use them to help or hinder your amateur sleuth. The stereotypical signs include: rapid eye blinking, fidgety hands and feet, and lack of eye contact. But an adept liar knows all of those signs and works to avoid them. Society has learned how to "behave" itself, hide true feelings, cultivate a role and then act the part.

However, many scientific studies have found that while there is no one clue that can be attributed to all people, a person can seldom put on a perfect performance no matter what their age, race, culture or sex. The subconscious is one area that is difficult to train and that is where the leaks occur. It shows in what we say, the way we say it and the way our bodies react. Lying is the verbal exchange of things not being what they seem.

Here's a list from law enforcement officials of what they watch for to determine if suspects are telling the truth or lying. You'll be able to use these traits as you create your characters.

Behavior Changes

Has this relaxed person become unusually hyper? Or has the normally animated suddenly become quite calm?

Speech Patterns

Is there a lot of hesitation? Broken sentences? Are they searching for words? Is their voice trembling? Are their answers becoming longer or shorter? It could be that they are inventing and embellishing events and scenarios.

If you combine *what* is being said with *how* it's being said, you might be able to gain more insight on the truth of the matter.

Abrupt, mid-sentence cutoffs happen when the speakers realize they've lost control over what they are saying. Those "um's" and "er's" they begin to mutter are needed to buy them time to form a coherent thought.

To write a character who is getting ready to project an image that's been well rehearsed, begin their dialogue with a flourish of throat clearings and coughs.

Volume, Tone, Words and Momentum

People often don't realize until it's too late that their voice has become higher or lower pitched, or that they've been speaking softer and slower or louder and faster than normal. Under stress, people also tend to use a vocabulary that is outside their normal scope and hope a bigger, more impressive word will add strength, impact and credibility to what they are saying.

Have your amateur take note of word slips; the most common are Freudian. People who are under stress and lying often inadvertently say more than "no." They embellish with adverbs and adjectives that can directly point out their lie. For example, the errant wife who claims that she's not having an affair with a young tennis pro when neither age nor occupation was ever mentioned.

Mannerisms and Body Language

Experts in the field of human behavior report the following mannerisms and body language that people display when they are lying. These are traits that a writer can apply to characters in various situations and that their amateur sleuth can witness.

People fidget, shuffle their feet and use lots of erratic hand motions. Studies show that women tend to "diddle" (make tiny movements) with their feet but stop when they are being deceptive. Men make few feet and leg movements but when they lie, the movements increase.

Liars have lots of nervous energy that is difficult to control because they become anxious about being caught in their lie. This manifests in sudden or repetitive movements, or doing unnecessary tasks.

Crossed arms over a chest often denotes that a person is trying to protect and defend themselves. Turning one's body away signals that a person wants to evade an issue. Locked ankles or clenched hands behind one's back can denote holding back strong feelings and emotions.

Physical Reactions

Sometimes fear of discovery will cause an actual physical reaction to the skin. Scientific studies have shown that the sides of the face redden slightly and a person's neck can turn blotchy. The Pinocchio Syndrome (granted, the nose won't grow) causes people to rub, stroke or pull at their nose to relieve stress. Under intense stress, the erectile tissues of the nasal passages become filled with blood and cause the nose to become extremely sensitive.

Writer's Research Note

Studies have shown that yawning, especially in people under the age of thirty, can be caused by stress and lying. Yawning is a tension reliever. The greater the tension, the bigger the yawn, sometimes with an added involuntary shudder of the person's body.

—"How to Tell When a Person Is Lying" by D. Glenn Foster and Mary Marshall, from the June 1994 issue of Good Housekeeping.

Looks Can Manipulate

Okay, call it sex. Call it lust. Call it animal attraction. But hasn't both the amateur and professional sleuth been tricked by someone's angelic beauty? Or that innocent male baby face?

The idea that beauty equates innocence can be a dangerous and deadly miscalculation. Don't believe the opposite, either— that the villain or villainess of the piece must be the one with the large nose, no neck, one eyebrow, constant snarl and hunchback.

Your amateur can use their looks to manipulate and gain information. A pair of thirty-eight's (no, not guns!) bursting from a Wonder Bra has been known to make even the tightest of lips begin to babble about all sorts of things. Depending on how far your female amateur is prepared to go to solve a case— or how comfortable you are with writing sex scenes—feminine wiles are a tried-and-true method of gaining information.

What of your male amateur? Suave and charming, caring and concerned, deliciously but deceitfully amorous and attentive. Oh, yes, he will certainly be able to get ladies of any age telling all their secrets.

Eye Movements

While blinking is a stereotypical response to the stress of lying, research has shown that many people are uncomfortable making eye contact at all. However, if a person would normally look you in the eye and doesn't . . .well, I suppose it could be new contact lenses!

Lying can only be successful if the person being lied to fails to really *see* and *hear* what's being said. That, of course, is *not* a problem for your amateur sleuth. Not only do they look and see, they listen and hear. They ask question after question because the longer people talk, the more mistakes they make. They are aware of those trivial details that deviate from normal behavior patterns. They ignore the carefully cultivated images that people project. They study both verbal and nonverbal signals. As you create the world your amateur inhabits, you also create the variations that signal your sleuth (and the reader) to "Watch out for this person. He's up to something; he's not telling me the truth." It's then up to you to decide if all these variations are true clues or red herrings.

''I Did It! I Confess!''

Is it possible to write a convincing scene that has your amateur sleuth actually coaxing a confession out of someone? According to criminal prosecutors, the following techniques have worked quite well in real-life situations. You can easily apply these techniques to your own writing to make the scene believable.

Create a False Sense of Security

Have your amateur use their disarming manner and charm to lull the culprit into a false sense of security. Then either gently coax the truth out of them or turn and pounce!

Just Enough Facts to Fake It

Your amateur can make the suspect believe that the truth is already known by relating enough facts that the suspect automatically fills in the missing pieces.

Good Cop/Bad Cop

The good cop/bad cop routine that they use on all those police shows really does work. One badgers, asks all the tough questions and even supplies wrong answers so that the suspect turns to mush. The other becomes all sympathetic, concerned and more humane so that the suspect begins to trust and tells the truth of what really happened. This technique can work especially well if your amateur has a partner in sleuthing.

Follow the Lie

The amateur sleuth who strongly believes that someone is lying will pursue that lie and defeat his opponent with relentless questions. That's why parents, especially mothers, can often trip up their children's lies, because they keep at it and ask question after question until slipups occur. Hmmm . . .maybe Mom is the best amateur sleuth!

Eavesdroppers—Cliché or Technique?

"I accidentally overheard Bill talking with his mistress and he told her where he'd buried his wife." Not only does that sentence tell the reader just about everything they need to know, but it is also the classic cliché. Overheard conversations—cliché. Eavesdroppers—cliché. Wait a minute. Does that mean that an author can never use these clichés?

No. Eavesdropping happens. From overheard conversations in movie theaters about critic reviews to listening to an argument in the office next door that reveals a corporate calamity, eavesdropping can be anywhere from an innocent occurrence to espionage.

Eavesdropping is exciting, fascinating and practiced by almost everyone. Fess up! We've all listened to someone else's conversation and wondered about the final outcome. This is a true puzzle. Most of the time, you never get closure, but you can have fun guessing what is really going on.

This is a wonderful habit to bestow on your amateur sleuth.

All sorts of plot possibilities open up when you use these two clichés to *your* advantage. Where can your amateur eavesdrop? In restaurants. In a shopping mall. In a physician's waiting room. On a bus. I guess a better question would be, where won't your amateur be able to eavesdrop? Eavesdropping can be amusing and helpful. Everyone likes being the person "in the know." Who better to be in the know than an amateur detective?

Non-Clichéd Eavesdropping

To use eavesdropping effectively in your writing, try adapting the following tips from some experts in the field: gossip columnists and private eyes. They report the best places to eavesdrop are crowded restaurants and movie theaters. Most people are relaxed and secure in this type of atmosphere, letting their guard down and their voices carry.

The third most interesting place to overhear conversations is the ladies' room. Even when it's crowded, women in rest rooms gossip and complain about the most amazing things! Little has to do with makeup and toiletries. (This will be a tough one for male amateur sleuths to try!)

If you have a scene where a suspect is on a pay phone, put your amateur sleuth on the pay phone next to them with their back facing the suspect. Make sure your amateur never reacts to anything that they overhear unless it's with a smug smile of success *after* the suspect leaves the scene.

Waiters and waitresses make wonderful sleuths because they have elevated eavesdropping to an art form. Just think of the conversations they hear while they invisibly refill water glasses, setup nearby tables, bring fresh bread or just stand next to a table while surveying the dining area to see who might need attention.

Is your amateur sleuth headed for the office Christmas party or a business cocktail party? What a perfect scene for sleuthing! Your amateur can mingle, munch and listen as they wander around *behind* the high-powered executive who is talking earnestly with another company's officer.

If you place your amateur at a crime scene but don't want them to get any help from the police, try using the following investigative reporter tactics to make a credible alternative.

Have your character stand close enough to witnesses or friends and family of the victim to hear them talking, but not so close that the sleuth is noticed. Make your amateur an unthreatening presence by having them turn away from the line of sight, look in another direction or pretend to be looking for something in a purse, their briefcase or their pockets.

Writer's Research Note

Experts report that emotional situations, where there's lots of tears, hugs or hysteria are where things happen and information is more forthcoming. You may want to write such a scene for your sleuth.

Mechanized Eavesdropping

Here are some other plot devices you can incorporate in your amateur detective novel that will provide both sleuth and reader with clues and information. Again, it will be up to you to determine if the information they provide will be of value.

Fax machines have proven to be a wonderful source of gossip. It's amazing the written messages that are sent across the phone lines without the thought of prying eyes or the fact that the office fax machine might not be dedicated to one individual.

Answering machines can also provide information for your amateur sleuth. If the machine answers the phone and starts recording a message, then is interrupted by a person picking up the receiver, most machines keep on recording. This makes a taped record of both sides of the conversations. If this two-sided conversation shows up on the victim's answering machine, this could be a valuable clue or may be a red herring for your sleuth.

The Information Superhighway is an electronic sieve, according to experts. So a writer can believably have a computer hacker (be it sleuth or villain) break into the most secure of systems, into someone's electronic mailbox or become a "lurker" who observes private computer bulletin boards.

Writer's Research Note

Many colleges and universities have posted warning no-
tices that state: "The privacy of computer activities cannot
be ensured."

Making Someone Eavesdrop on Your Sleuth

Depending on what your amateur detective does for a living,
they can find themselves on the other end of eavesdropping.
Electronic spying in the workplace has become quite widespread. Courts have ruled in favor of the companies, for the
most part, because the only relevant existing federal law is one
that forbids employers' knowingly listening to workers' personal phone conversations.

An unscrupulous employer has always been able to gain
access to a worker's office to read phone messages or go through
paper and computer files. High-tech equipment makes it even
easier to acquire information about anyone using a computer
terminal, electronic telephone console, scanners, cash registers
and other normal office machinery.

Current estimates suggest that over forty million workers
are under surveillance on any given day. That leaves any amateur sleuth vulnerable and they don't even know it. Here are the
techniques actually used by companies to spy on workers:

Monitoring Computers

Everything an employee does on a computer can be accessed by the company. Some workers are even required to log
on and off their computer systems when they take a coffee break
or use the bathroom. An employer knows every second the employee isn't being productive. Can this type of computer monitoring be deleted? No. With today's advances in both software
and hardware technology, the number of keystrokes that are
typed, how many errors are made and what the computer screen
looks like can be recorded and made available to the boss.

The Telephone

While federal law prohibits personal phone calls from being tapped, most employers are within their rights to monitor business-related calls by their workers. This is quite widespread among consumer-based service industries such as catalogue sales, insurance, credit card offers and airline reservation clerks. In fact, a person will often be made aware of the situation with a verbal cue: "Your call may be monitored by a supervisor." Be aware, however, that *all calls* are probably being monitored and, more than likely, recorded.

Thinking of calling in sick just to get a day off for fun? Think again. The boss might have one of the new voice-stress analyzers attached to his phone. The stress analyzer is capable of detecting emotional levels in voices in the same way a lie detector works on blood pressure. A person's tone may reflect that they're not as ill as they claim.

Voice Mail and E-Mail

Voice mail is a pretty standard fixture in most companies. A password does not guarantee security. A person's password is on file just as a commonsense business precaution in case of illness or death. Voice mailbox messages are always available for review.

E-mail—the paperless, fast way to communicate via computer—is also not secure. Don't ever complain about a job, benefits, personal problems and so on because those notes can be "caught" and read by others.

Candid Camera

With today's technology, video cameras can be as tiny as a fingertip with an even smaller microphone. Businesses have installed them in company cafeterias, lounges, offices and even rest rooms. *No. It is not illegal.*

Big Brother is watching how much socializing is being done on the job, who's being talked about and who's stealing supplies or rifling co-workers' purses. It's not all negative monitoring. Video cameras have kept surveillance on bank clerks, ATM machines, cash registers—all with their eye on protecting individuals from harm.

Writer's Research Note

Police have been able to use the videotape from outdoor ATM cash machines to view what went on in a wider area than just at the machine.

Gadgets Galore

Here are some unique gadgets that a writer can make use of in the amateur sleuth novel. Have your sleuth take another look at an **electronic key** used in office buildings. Individual key-cards have their own codes that register whenever a person opens a lock.

That **name badge** isn't as harmless as it appears. It can house a transmitter that emits a signal to a company's central computer system, which makes it possible for the person wearing the badge to be tracked throughout the building.

Pens do more than write these days. They can also be fitted with transmitters that let others listen and record conversations even when a person isn't at work.

Making Your Sleuth Spy-Proof

If you choose to plot an amateur sleuth novel in the corporate venue, you need to know the legalities of the business world. Workers cannot expect the same right of privacy in the workplace that they have in their homes. The laws have not kept up with technology and lawmakers are bowing to business lobbying groups that say such legislation is not necessary.

Employers argue that they have the right to protect their company's interests and prevent unscrupulous workers from taking advantage of their office situations by engaging in illegal activities. Disgruntled employees have been known to sabotage companies or pass along confidential information to competitors. They also point out that such spying protects their workers and enhances their on-the-job safety. If an employee becomes aware that they are being monitored and objects, they can be fired for insubordination.

Now that you understand that there is no legal recourse to

combat employer spying, what believable precautions can your amateur sleuth take? Here's what they are doing in the real world:

1. Computer and E-mail passwords are changed on a weekly or even daily basis. While this is not foolproof, it makes it more difficult for someone to access material.

2. Make sure computer monitor screens don't show material. Employees need to educate themselves about computer security and learn how to use company software to their advantage.

Advances in technology and communications have made the world a relatively small place. Never say or write anything you don't want the world to know.

Pretexts

One time-honored tradition used by writers of amateur detective novels is to develop a pretext that allows the sleuth to gain information that will help them solve the crime.

Here are some devious but totally legal techniques that you can employ for your character:

Telephone sweet talk: Lead your amateur to the telephone where they can hide behind a cloak of invisibility and skillfully acquire information such as names and addresses by becoming: a telephone or utility company repair person asking questions to clear up problems; or a delivery person getting ready to deliver flowers or food.

Your sleuth could also claim to be an associate's temporary secretary in need of phone and address information from their Rolodex or ask to have a previous fax or other documents retransmitted to another number because of technical problems.

Let your amateur cajole having duplicate fax information retransmitted to their machines by hotels or businesses by using a pretext such as: "My boss, Mr. Henderson, stayed in your hotel last week and has lost his receipt. Could you please fax him another copy at . . .?"

In person: Take a page from many a mystery author's book and turn your amateur into a master or mistress of disguise and illusion. Your sleuth can become that delivery person carrying flowers, fruit or office supplies to gain physical access. Delivery people, in or out of uniform, are often an invisible part of the business day's agenda. Then have them snoop around looking for clues, seeing what information is lying on a desk in an unoccupied office or browsing through an open file drawer.

Don't overlook adding *trash* to your novel. Archaeologists have been researching trash as material evidence to help define societies through the ages of man. Trash, from office wastebaskets to the outside garbage can, is the perfect place for your amateur to hunt for clues. Garbage, by the way, is fair game. It's perfectly legal to pick up someone else's trash at the curb, so supply your sleuth with a pair of rubber gloves and have them dig in.

What items will your amateur be looking for? Discarded food and drink containers; correspondence that can provide return addresses, phone numbers and postage markings as well as the information they contain.

Writers can also use garbage as an innovative way to extend a character's (both amateur sleuth and others) profile for the reader. A bag full of junk food containers, candy bar wrappers and porno magazines describes a totally different character than a bag filled with vegetable peelings, rice, crushed pasta cartons and fashion magazines.

Credit card receipts and bank statements provide highly useful information for detectives both in the real world and on the printed page. The credit card companies provide automated 1-800 phone numbers that will access account information when the account number and, usually, a zip code is punched in. Banking information is accessible in the same fashion. Dial the bank's 1-800 number, press in the account number and listen to the menu choices.

Forewarned Is Forearmed

In 1994, Americans spent over four hundred million dollars on home and personal security devices. Safety product catalogues have become a burgeoning industry. While amateur sleuths are known for turning the most insignificant objects into deadly weapons, here are some of the latest in personal and home protection that you might find useful to include in your mystery:

Writer's Research Note

It is illegal to take documents and other discarded trash material from a crime scene. If it's cordoned off with police tape, stay away until it's fair game.

- Body safes. Hide valuables in a Bra Stash, or leg and waist safes. The latter are very inconspicuous and nearly impossible for a mugger to grab. One interesting note: Communications Control Systems (CCS) can turn a mink coat into bulletproof armor for about $3,600.
- At home or on the road, try the Door Club or the Jammer, which can be used on sliding doors as well.
- Want the benefit of a dog without the care? Try Watchdog. It uses radar to detect moving objects up to sixteen feet away and then begins to bark like a frantic Doberman.
- There's a host of infrared motion detectors available that sound alarms when their coverage area is breached.
- You might like to arm your amateur detective with a personal safety alarm that emits an earsplitting decibel shriek. Or one of the new high-security flashlights that can temporarily blind an attacker.
- Pepper sprays and Mace can blind and choke for up to twenty minutes. A Spotlight can blind with light, pepper spray and dye. There's even an ampoule that's recommended for joggers that, when crushed, can make the person smell like a skunk. Very unappetizing to a would-be rapist or attacker. There is an odor-eliminating solution that is also provided.

Writer's Research Note

Make sure you know the local and state laws regarding the use of pepper sprays and Mace for the locale in which you've set your mystery. In some cities and states, they are illegal!

- There's always Safe-T-Man—a stuffed, six-foot, 180-pound doll with a face guaranteed to scare. He comes with a tote bag for easy carrying.
- Want something a bit more genteel but equally as effective for your sleuth? Hair spray will temporarily blind a foe; a sharp nail file or maybe even a penknife can double as weapons and break-in/break-out tools. Hat pins, umbrellas and brick-filled reticules have been stock-in-trade tools for amateur sleuths for many years.

Now that we have discussed some of the techniques and equipment you can use to help your amateur sleuth solve cases in a believable manner, let's take a look at what other expert information is available for constructing your mystery novel.

F O U R

RESOURCES AND INFORMATION FOR THE WRITER AND THE AMATEUR SLEUTH

Bodies, Bodies Everywhere!

For the amateur detective, bodies seem to be everywhere. They've been found in belfries and mansions; face up in herb gardens and face down in kitty's litter box. The deceased have been centerpieces at catered affairs or looking a bit more than drunk holding a mint julep. From Alaska to Zambia, if there's a body to find, you can bet that the amateur sleuth will be the first one on the scene, become the prime suspect or know for certain that the prime suspect is absolutely innocent.

How is it possible that the amateur keeps tripping over bodies when the crime rate is at an all-time low? According to the FBI's statistics for January through June 1995, violent crimes reported to law enforcement agencies in the United States decreased 5 percent. Murder dropped a record 12 percent, the biggest decline in thirty-five years. Murders were even down

17 percent in cities with a population of a million or more.

However, the murder rate increased right in the amateur sleuth's backyard—small town America and the suburbs. Here, the uniform crime reports show a 12 percent increase in murder in the 100,000 to 249,999 population group, and a 13 percent increase in the 25,000 to 49,999 population group. As a whole, violent crimes in the suburbs increased 2 percent and 3 percent in rural areas.

Criminologists point out that people are most vulnerable in the place where they ought to feel the safest: at home. For the amateur, home is more than a house covered by bricks or aluminum siding. Home becomes a world that Agatha Christie likened to a medieval morality play; a world where people's lives are dominated by lust, power, greed and lies.

The calm and peaceful surface of home is a facade that covers intimate, destructive and frightening secrets. To survive in this world, the amateur needs to channel their great intellect along with their other natural abilities into accessing the multitudes of legal information available. They have to work smart in gaining information about the victim or suspects because they are at the distinct disadvantage of not having crime scene data available. Unless they have a friend in the police department, the amateur doesn't have the facts of the autopsy report, know whose fingerprints were found on the murder weapon or know what the DNA lab test results were. While the police are able to get warrants to search for evidence or subpoena phone and bank records, the amateur has to rely on ingenuity, legwork and pretexts to come up with who really dunnit.

To make an amateur sleuth sound credible on the printed page, a writer needs to know how to find out practically anything about anybody or any body. Frankly, it's not that difficult. In fact, it's almost frightening to discover the amount of information that is accessible to just about anyone.

The following is being written from the point of view of the amateur detective. This will make it easier for you to adapt it directly to your sleuth and adjust the amount of data you wish to use.

How to Detect Like a Detective

A police detective has the full resources of the law enforcement community to access when information is needed about a suspect or the deceased. Private detectives and amateur sleuths can usually obtain the same information, but they have to get it from different sources and it won't be instantaneous.

A detective and your amateur sleuth should begin a search by writing down everything known about a person, no matter how obvious or trivial it may seem. List their first, middle and last name; nickname; current and previous addresses; phone number; birth date; current job; and social security number, if known. Then the *legwork* really begins with the search of public records.

Public Records

This is information about people, businesses and organizations that is available legally to anyone without benefit of subpoena or fabricated story. There is enough public information available about people, their true identities, their past and their activities that your sleuth should be able to investigate any suspicions and act on them or lay them to rest. Public information is available from various government agencies and industry databases.

At the city level, your amateur will be able to access records concerning traffic court, utilities, building permits and business and professional licenses.

County records include voter and auto registrations, marriage and divorce records, property tax and deed information, civil court actions, business information and some criminal histories.

The state maintains business incorporation papers, notary registers, motor vehicle registrations, assumed name information, criminal arrest and conviction filings and licensing registration.

From the federal government comes military records, Social Security information, bankruptcy procedures, immigration information, passports, international commerce and other business documentation.

The court system keeps information on civil and criminal cases in their jurisdictions.

The County Office Building

If the suspect has lived in the area for any amount of time, the county office building will be your amateur's first stop on the paper trail chase. They don't need to bother thinking up a clever story; just tell the clerk what records are wanted. Most can be found on either microfiche or computer databases.

Board of Elections

With the exception of Alabama and Hawaii, where there is no access, and North Carolina, where there is limited access, voter registration information is available to anyone, although the regulations of each state may change. What will your sleuth find? If the person is a registered voter, on file will be their correct legal name, current address, past address from voting in other areas, marital status, date and place of birth and Social Security number along with their official signature. One other extra perk: often the home phone number is noted, even when it's an unlisted number. If the particular person isn't registered, your sleuth is savvy enough to check to see if their spouse or children are registered. Birth information is a valuable tool.

Recorder's Office

The recorder's office is where your amateur will find birth certificates, marriage licenses and an index of local business names that will be cross-indexed under the owner's names. Marriage licenses show a wealth of information including: birth dates for both bride and groom, parents' names, any previous marriages, both Social Security numbers, witnesses names and, sometimes, driver's license numbers or passport identification if one is a foreigner.

Court Clerk

The county clerk's office holds *civil court* proceedings that will show if the subject has ever filed a civil lawsuit against someone or had one filed against them. *Municipal court* is where the records on evictions, lawsuits for small-claims cases, misdemeanors and traffic violations are filed. *Superior court* files contain information on felony and criminal convictions. *Probate court* will provide information if they've ever been named in a will. *Family court* provides records on divorce settlements, custody, restraining orders and payment of child support. *Federal district court* is where any bankruptcy filings are shown.

Criminal history records are all computerized by name and date of birth. Even the FBI's National Crime Information Center (NCIC), which collects information from across the country, uses the person's name and birth date to record information.

Criminal Records

If your suspect has a criminal record, the following will be in their file jackets: the type of criminal charge, pretrial information, conviction record and where they were remanded. The clerk's file will also reveal information regarding parole, probation, fines, penalties and awarded restitution.

Pretrial notes cover interviews with the defendant, their personal and employment history plus any prior criminal charges. If the person applied for a bond, the agency is noted. From the bondsman, your amateur will be able to find out if the defendant skipped on their bond and had to be located as well as learn reference names that could lead to more information.

Civil Records

Most people will never be charged with a crime, but many will become part of a civil lawsuit, either as a witness, plaintiff or defendant. Statistics show that your sleuth's chance of finding information about someone in civil records is more than ten times greater than in criminal records. Often, there's little civility about what's recorded in civil court proceedings because most are filed to recover debts and/or damages from people or businesses.

Small-claims or municipal courts deal with a set low-dollar limit on claims that include bad checks, nonpayment of small debts and minor damages. Most of the time, these actions are filed without benefit of lawyers and are decided by a judge.

District and superior state courts, using judges and/or juries, decide larger financial damage cases including personal injury and divorce actions. These are often more complicated cases that require discovery motions and lawyers.

The federal district court hears cases involving interstate commerce, antitrust, civil rights, international business and federal contracts, as well as many other federally related cases and any incidents that involve or occur on federal property.

Records from the federal and state courts are quite extensive. Have your amateur explore pretrial depositions, background information on all parties, names and addresses of subpoenaed witnesses and all the claims to prove civil damages.

Detailed financial information can be found in most divorce case records. Don't forget to have your sleuth look for a copy of the property settlement agreement, which will list all assets and liabilities that were in place at that time. This agreement shows all assets, no matter what state or country they are located in, plus any inheritances and business assets.

Other Lawsuits

Your amateur detective needs to look for files that detail personal injury, fraud and "deadbeat" cases. If the suspect has a history of filing personal injury and insurance claims, you'll be able to read the depositions and descriptions of the injuries along with any financial settlement.

Fraud claims are notably well documented and specific in their charges of activities. Normally a person uses the same fraudulent pattern over and over. It becomes their *MO* or modus operandi. Court records list witnesses, co-conspirators and who was defrauded. These may become new leads that you'll be able to further pursue.

Creditors who file financial claims against "deadbeats" provide detailed information in their records. Let your detective view old financial statements, a listing of assets and business ventures, plus a history of past addresses on the person.

Bankruptcy

Bankruptcy actions are held in federal court and often listed in the business section of major newspapers. Some days it appears as if everyone and every business is filing for protection under the provisions in the Chapter 11 Federal Bankruptcy Act. In 1991, the United States Supreme Court ruled that both businesses and individuals could continue to operate while they reorganized in hopes of paying their creditors in the future.

Bankruptcy records show the names and addresses of all creditors as well as the amount of money they are owed, discovery motions, specific rules so that creditors can maintain their legal rights and claims, plus a list of the company's or person's debts and assets at the time of the filing. These records are useful in determining someone's past or present business and financial health as well as their character in paying off creditors and possible fraud in hiding assets. Con men survive and become wealthy when people blindly believe what they say and never check out their history.

Property Records

The mansion in the country, the condo in the city, the chalet at the ski resort, the yacht, the three cars, the personal jet—if it sounds too good to be true, it usually is. That's why real estate and personal property records are available for your perusal.

Real estate records will show if that mansion is really owned or rented, mortgaged to the hilt with assorted liens or free and clear. The files will show the deed of trust and the amount of debt, the legal description and value of the property, and any lien holders. Your amateur can learn who previous owners of the property were and any activity concerning the property, from where utilities are buried to how the ground percolates.

If your sleuth finds the real estate records complex and confusing, they won't be alone. The amateur knows how to go one step further and ask for help from a real estate agent who will be able to make sense of the documentation.

Tax Assessor Records

Most tax assessor information has been computerized and consolidated, so that it becomes very easy to access a variety of records in one place—the county clerk's office. In fact, many areas have their records open certain weeks of the year so that property owners can see if their taxes are higher than their neighbors who own a duplicate house.

On the real estate tax rolls, examine the legal description, plat, lot, street number, survey records, improvements, permits, the assessed valuation on a specific piece of property and if the property owner has paid the current tax bill.

Writer's Research Note

Remember, the occupant of the house or the person paying the taxes may not be the owner. If the property is leased or rented, make sure your amateur checks on the true ownership and the possibility of a sublease.

In some counties, personal property tax is charged on boats, cars, campers and so on. You'll be able to check on the true value and ownership of these items.

Utility Records

Have your sleuth make a phone call to the utility company to find out the name of the person who is being billed at a certain address.

Probate Records

When your amateur needs to find out if someone really inherited millions from his great-grandfather, send them to inspect the probate records. The files provide grandpa's will and the inheritance information that shows how the assets were dispersed.

Department of Motor Vehicles

Public access to licensed driver information is fully available in most states, with no access in California, Montana and Oklahoma. Limited access is available to those with authority or police in Alaska, Arizona, Arkansas, Georgia, Hawaii, Michigan, Nevada, North Carolina, North Dakota, Pennsylvania, Virginia and Washington.

What will your sleuth find? A photo that will establish a visual identity and detail the physical characteristics of weight, height, hair, eye color and race. The DMV can provide information on driving records and restrictions, and, by using the license plate number, you can find the legal owner of a vehicle.

Department of Vital Statistics

This agency compiles data on birth, death and marriage from cities and counties around the state. Copies of birth certificates, unless they're your own, have become nearly impossible to duplicate because of the high trafficking in illegal documentation that has gone on for years.

Military Records

Military records are available to the public using the Freedom of Information Act. To locate military personnel on a base where they are currently or previously stationed, contact the base's public affairs office and ask for the Freedom of Information officer. They will be able to give your sleuth all the information the law allows. Each branch of the armed forces also has their own locator service based in Washington, DC. It will help if your amateur detective has a Social Security number or other military information.

Since the Vietnam War, many organizations have been formed to help servicemen and/or their families locate each other, share information and share memories. Depending on the branch of military service, your amateur could contact the locator at the U.S. Soldier's and Airmen's Home or try the U.S. Office of Military History.

What if your amateur detective needs to check out a pilot? The FAA (Federal Aviation Administration) locator is also in Washington, DC and will be able to tell if your subject is or was a pilot, their flying qualifications, where their last required physical exam took place and when it's up for renewal, plus the usual information revealing current address, Social Security number, date of birth and physical description. The FAA houses detailed information on all types of aircraft, the last known owner and address of a specific airplane and maintenance schedule, as well as information on plane crashes and accidents.

Social Security Numbers

The Internal Revenue Service requires that every person over the age of two must have their own Social Security number. Some states use that as a person's driver's license number as well. A Social Security number is yours for life and can't be changed or duplicated. The nine numbers are coded and can be a valuable clue for finding out where a person was first issued their card. The first three numbers indicate the state or territory where the card was issued. The next two digits are group numbers that further break down the state or territory location, and the final four digits form a serial number within the group.

How could you use this information? You might, for example, write a scene where your sleuth has been suspicious about a man who is dating their rich aunt. He claims to be a "son of the South" and a scion of a wealthy old Virginia family. Your sleuth could just happen to get a look at this man's Virginia driver's license and see that the first three numbers of the license are 135. If he's a born-and-bred Virginian, the driver's license numbers are also Social Security numbers and 135 happens to be allocated to New Jersey! The chart on page 79 is an abbreviated Social Security table for the first three numbers that your amateur sleuth can use to find out more information about a suspect. The numbers on the chart show the range of first three numbers used in that state; for example, Alabama uses 416 *through* 424.

Other Leads

College registrar's offices will tell your sleuth if a subject is an alumnus. State licensing or certification boards will tell you if they are licensed to practice a profession and whether anyone has filed any complaints. Professional organizations and unions also maintain membership directories, on both the state and

Social Security Prefixes

State	Number	State	Number
Alabama..................	416-424	Alaska.........................	574
Arizona...................	526-527	Arizona...................	600-601
Arkansas	429-432	California	545-573
California	602-620	California	621-626
Colorado	521-524	Connecticut	040-049
Delaware.................	221-222	District of Columbia	577-579
Florida....................	261-267	Florida....................	589-595
Georgia...................	252-260	Hawaii....................	575-576
Idaho	518-519	Illinois....................	318-361
Indiana	303-309	Indiana	310-317
Iowa......................	478-485	Kansas....................	509-515
Kentucky.................	400-407	Louisiana.................	433-439
Maine.....................	004-007	Maryland.................	212-220
Massachusetts.............	010-034	Michigan.................	362-386
Minnesota.................	468-477	Mississippi...............	425-428
Mississippi...............	587-588	Missouri..................	486-500
Montana...................	516-517	Nebraska	505-508
Nevada	530	New Hampshire	001-003
New Jersey...............	135-158	New Mexico..................	525
New York	050-134	North Carolina................	232
North Carolina............	237-246	North Dakota	501-502
Ohio......................	268-302	Oklahoma	440-448
Oregon	540-544	Pennsylvania.............	159-211
Rhode Island..............	035-038	South Carolina............	247-251
South Dakota	503-504	Tennessee	408-415
Texas	449-467	Utah	528-529
Vermont..................	008-009	Virginia....................	223-231
Washington	531-539	West Virginia	232-234
Wisconsin.................	387-399	Wyoming....................	520
Unassigned 000;729-799;627-699			

national levels, so it's easy to ascertain if someone is a member of the American Bar Association or American Medical Association, or is an RN, LPN, CPA, steam fitter, plumber or longshoreman, to name a few.

What if your amateur needs to learn more about a business? Have them begin by checking out their permits with the city. Next stop is the county clerk or state records office to access their Uniform Commercial Code (UCC) records. UCC records show if their business equipment is used as collateral.

Libraries

There is no better place for an amateur sleuth to rely on the kindness of others than in a library. Today's library is a warehouse of technology with everything from computer terminals networked to a wide variety of on-line information sources to extended CD-ROM reference material. Most reference librarians are quite amenable when it comes to helping hunt down information. Don't just limit your sleuth to the public library. The same helpful librarians can be found in county law libraries, and at colleges and universities. The latter are very useful for researching special collections information.

The library will provide your amateur with easy access to items such as:

- Reverse telephone directory, which provides a name to the phone number; a 1-800 Number Directory; and phone directories from major cities
- Who's Who—in all its manifestations—where you can complete your background and other identifying information on your subject
- Business information like Dun & Bradstreet, Standard and Poor's, and Moody's
- State business directories that include businesses by city, yellow page categories, major employers and manufacturers by city and product
- "The American Business Disc," a CD-ROM that contains ten million businesses that lets you search by company name, yellow page headings, zip code, city and state

- Manufacturers Directory lists more than 120,000 companies that have twenty-five or more employees and what their products are
- Big Business Directory contains comprehensive information on the top 140,000 companies that employ one hundred or more people as well as profiles on 300,000 top executives and directors
- Credit Reference Directory that has business credit references on more than ten million U.S. businesses
- Pro-Quest Periodical Abstracts Library that encapsulates articles from hundreds of sources over a ten-year period and provides a printout
- City, county, state and federal indexes, source information, guidelines, contacts
- Interstate library lending and, often, access to large college libraries if you're looking for hard-to-find research volumes
- Computer on-line access to the Internet and World Wide Web (more on that later)
- Don't forget the biggest research library, the Library of Congress. Write to the Library of Congress, National Reference Service, Washington, DC 20540 and ask for their free brochure that instructs on how to use the stacks and access information. They are on the Internet at **http://www.loc.gov/** where they are making various collections of photos and manuscripts available

Having your amateur sleuth access publicly known and used avenues of information that readers can identify with makes the character more appealing and convincing. It also makes the reader believe that they, too, are equal to being an amateur detective because they now know the exact steps to take to check someone out!

Contact Guides

Many universities and colleges publish directories called *Contact Guides*, which is a listing of faculty and staff members who are prepared to share their knowledge on a wide variety of topics. One of the best is *Purdue's Contacts*, which is available from Purdue University's Office of Publications. You don't have to create a super genius amateur sleuth, all you have to do is have your character tap into the great intellects at universities and get information on diverse topics, from popcorn breeding to veterinary virology and from toxic fungi to thinking processes.

Writer's Research Note

Your amateur sleuth isn't the only one who can use this type of information. You can make excellent use of it as research material for your entire novel.

Computer Programs

If your amateur sleuth is at all computer smart, they can own CD-ROM information software programs that hold a bonanza of information. The topics are as diverse as the white and yellow pages of the entire country to medical programs that can morph, or age, a person's features.

Telephone Help

Your sleuth can let their fingers do a lot of quick investigating by taking advantage of the many 1-800 numbers (and recently, 1-888 numbers) that provide a credible source for getting facts. If you're writing a financial theme, it is perfectly logical for your sleuth to check on a broker with the National Association of Securities Dealers (NASD). Their computerized database is called the Central Registration Depository and it maintains records about the disciplinary histories of all brokers and securities firms.

Using a medical theme and want to have your sleuth check out a doctor? The nationally recognized American Board of Medical Specialties (ABMS) is where they can check on whether a doctor is certified by a recognized board and whether the certification is in the specialty they are claiming.

Expert Information

Where does an amateur sleuth go when they need to know about investigative or even illegal techniques? There's a wealth of material available to turn an amateur into a near-professional. (And provide you with probably more in-depth information than you might want.)

Start by sending your sleuth to the newsstand to buy magazines aimed at the professional private investigator, such as *P.I. Magazine* or *True Crime* or *Soldier of Fortune*. There's also specialized bookstores, like SpyTech out of Canada, which sell specific how-to guides that cover such topics as how to: find anyone, find facts, access on-line information sources, be an expert at reading body language, learn tricks of the burglar trade like picking locks, or driving techniques for escape. There are also practical guides for businesses like how to stop internal losses, retail security measures and business privacy.

Another excellent source of reference material for both writer and sleuth, if the college or university offers criminal justice and private investigation classes, is a campus bookstore. Here you'll usually find the most up-to-date volumes on crime scene investigation, criminal evidence and procedures, criminal behavior, private detective's and investigator's course manuals.

If you're the type of writer, or amateur sleuth, who'd rather let their fingers do the walking, the next chapter will fit you to a T.

F I V E

THE INFORMATION SUPERHIGHWAY

All detectives, amateur or professional, should heed these words from the famous Sherlock Holmes: "It is of the highest importance in the art of detection to be able to recognize out of a number of facts which are incidental and which are vital. It is a capital mistake to theorize before one has that data."

Those statements are just as true today as when Sir Arthur Conan Doyle wrote them for Holmes to say at the turn of the century. As a writer, this is a credo that both you and your amateur sleuth should live by.

But where does a writer go to find information for use in creating the mystery novel and making the characterization of their amateur sleuth believable? The newest road to facts and data is the *information superhighway.*

Accessing Facts and Data

The information superhighway is where you and your amateur sleuth can expand your knowledge and contacts to global proportions. All that is needed is a computer, modem and mouse. If neither you nor your amateur sleuth have a computer, head back to the public library where most offer free Internet connections to the public. Their simple how-to instructions will turn you and your character into professional Internet surfers. What if the public library doesn't have on-line access? Try contacting a local high school, college or university and see what type of deal can be worked out using their computer systems.

The following pages will be useful in learning how to increase your knowledge by accessing up-to-date research sources. There are very few writers who can just sit down and start creating a novel from the knowledge that they inherently possess. The more information that can be acquired on a subject, the more believable the writing becomes. Again, you are sharing with the reader the logic of a certain situation. If believability is high, then so is the credibility of both your plot (making it shockingly real) and actions of your amateur sleuth (making them logical). The information superhighway makes gathering information about anything extremely easy for both writer and sleuth. This is not to say a writer has to create an amateur sleuth that is a computer nerd or even computer literate. But since the public has entered into a love affair with the Internet and World Wide Web, why not use this to your advantage? By making your sleuth have another common bond with the reader, this helps solidify that important one-on-one connection between reader and character.

This chapter is being addressed to both writer and amateur sleuth. As a writer, we will guide you to some interesting research stops that will enable you to write more effectively. You can, in turn, show your amateur sleuth accessing this same information to help them solve the crime.

The Internet

The Internet is a network of networks connecting your computer to computers around the world. Governments, schools, companies and individuals make information available to anyone who wants it.

One of your best tools for finding all this global data is a

Author Michael Wolf

"The Internet is similar to what the library was one hundred years ago. It represents who we are, how we act, transact business and engage in relationships. The Internet is about information empowerment. I think it will change world culture."
—*Investors Business Daily*, 9/21/95

Who's on the Internet?

- 37 million people in the United States and Canada—17 percent of the total population.
- 24 million are adults
- 33 percent are women
- 50 percent are between ages 16 and 34
- They spend 5½ hours a week surfing the Net
- 64 percent have a four-year college degree
- 22 percent have incomes over $80,000

source such as the *Internet Yellow Pages*, which gives you the nomenclature for over twenty thousand electronic entries and thirteen thousand newspapers, web sites, contacts and so on. Or you can use magazines like *Online Access* and *PC Novice* where each issue focuses on where to find Internet and on-line services for a specific topic. If you want to jump right in, surf to **Excite** where you'll find reviews of nearly thirty thousand sites at **http://www.atext.com**, or surf to **Yahoo!**, which is a Web site listing topics at **http://www.yahoo.com**. The most exhaustive search tool is produced by Lycos Inc. and located at **http://www.lycos.com**. Its indexes reference over eleven million Web sites. It uses a match-any-term/match-all-terms option. Another favorite is **Infoseek** at **http://www.infoseek.com** where you can type questions in plain English (Who is Dorothy L. Sayers?) to get a listing of relevant Web sites. Infoseek is the only tool that allows you to browse through the part of the Internet called Usenet, where all the discussion groups are located.

The easiest way to connect to the Internet is via a commercial on-line service such as America Online, CompuServe, Prodigy or MSN (The MicroSoft Network). They are all mini-Internets that provide news, weather and sports; financial and travel information; reference material like on-line encyclopedias, magazines and cookbooks; network television news; libraries; and even the Bible, plus discussion and forum groups. You can also subscribe to a no-frills Internet provider in just about every corner of the country.

The four most popular areas of the Internet are E-mail, chat lines, Usenet groups and the World Wide Web.

E-Mail

Electronic mail allows you to write and send letters instantly around the globe to other E-mail addresses.

Chat Lines

Welcome to the party! Chat lines allow you to communicate live with people around the world by typing messages and receiving responses. Virtual chat rooms are becoming quite popular. You pick a figure to represent yourself and then visit various *rooms* that feature discussions on a variety of topics like health, food and politics. You'll also encounter other figures as you walk from room to room. (What a useful tool for a writer or amateur sleuth who, for example, decides to mix murder with food and doesn't know how to boil water!) Visit Worlds Inc's Worlds Chat at **http://www.worlds.net** for a demonstration of a virtual chat world.

Usenet

These are newsgroups or discussion forums where people share more in-depth discussions on topics. You can read *postings*, or messages, from other users and leave your own thoughts and ideas posted for thousands to see.

World Wide Web

The Web is a collection of more than fifty thousand sites or pages that have been set up by anyone about everything imaginable. Universities, archives, museums and the private sector upload volumes of previously obscure or new information daily. Whether it's fact or fiction, music, historical documents, corporate

---

Writer's Research Note

There are several hundred criminal justice bulletin boards nationally that disseminate public information, link prosecutors, judges and court officials and provide one of the best crime preventive efforts going. This is a perfect area to surf to when you need to know how to create believable dialogue for a law enforcement character.

PR, pop culture, the impossible or the improbable, it can be found on the World Wide Web. Through the Web and a few clicks on your mouse, you can access information, in English, from a university in Spain or read last year's *London Times* from the archives in England.

Each state and most major cities have Web sites that will give you name, address and contact information to access everything from earthquake hazards to missing persons clearinghouses.

Here are some samples of what you'll find on-line. **Warning:** Everything is not free and ordering information on-line with a credit card is still a risky venture. It is better to get a telephone number and place your order that way.

http://artsedge.kennedy-center.org Artsedge is the national arts and education information center.

http://lcweb.loc.gov/homepage/lchp.html This is the Library of Congress site and their legislative information site, THOMAS, is at **http://thomas.loc.gov/**.

http://nhic-nt.health.org/odphp.htm National Health Information Center (NHIC) is an excellent government resource site featuring toll-free numbers of organizations that provide health-related information. There are currently over five hundred health-related electronic chat rooms on the Internet. **Warning:** Not everyone is a legitimate doctor, so practicing medical fraud in cyberspace has become very easy.

http://public.att.com/bnet/services/dink.html Visit the *Washington Post's Digital Ink* site for a variety of on-line services and international access and download their software to make exploring easier.

http://seawifs.gsfc.nasa.gov/ocean_planet.html This is the National Museum of Natural History.

http://the-tech.mit.edu/Shakespeare/works.html Sift through the complete works of Shakespeare at this site.

http://www.amex.com American Stock Exchange Web site includes the daily stock market summary, information about equity options and derivatives, news reports and an information exchange that links users to other financial data.

http://www.atcon.com/HPD/hpd.htm Halifax Police Department provides information for the local community, news about unsolved crimes and contests for Net surfers.

http://www.bizmag.com The Biz is devoted to entertainment media information and book publishing.

http://www.census.gov/ For more demographics, tap into Bureau of the Census.

http://www.city.net City.Net is an enormous collection of links to countries, states, provinces, counties and cities around the world. Try **http://wings.buffalo.edu/world/vt2/** for a map interface to City.Net.

http://www.dejanews.com DejaNews Research Services will search newsgroups using keywords for information retrieval.

http://www.delorme.com/ This is where you'll find Delorme Mapping.

http://www.digiwis.com/ Digital Wisdom/Globeshots has stunning photos and graphics that you can download.

http://www.dtic.dla.mil/defenselink DefenseLink is where the Department of Defense has organized all its branches geographically. The Web page links to each branch and fact files.

http://www.eff.org/pub/Legal/Cases/FCC_v_Pacifica/fcc_v_pacifica.decision Use the Electronic Frontier Foundation legal archives if you need to understand legal doctrines.

http://www.elibrary.com/ The Electronic Library has a huge database with more than one thousand full-text newspapers, magazines and academic journals; plus images, reference books, literature and art.

http://www.fednews.com Federal News Service provides full text transcripts of government speeches; daily news coverage of the White House, Congress, congressional hearings, the Supreme Court, Federal Reserve and UN; and there's a daybook that notes schedules of events and translation services, including one with Russia.

http://www.fedworld.gov/#usgovt or **http://www.fedworld.gov/** FedWorld is the most popular government Web site where you'll find a massive alphabetical listing of World Wide Web sites plus all 120 government sites.

http://www.fedworld.gov/ntis/ntishome.html National Technical Information Service (on Telnet: **fedworld**) gathers and sells technological, scientific and business demographics and research. They provide a research database of searchable information that is constantly updated. Surf them for a variety of information.

http://www.guardian.co.uk/ Try the *Guardian* newspaper to check on terrorist acts.

http://www.hoovers.com Hoover's Online reference site lists just about everything you need to know about 8,500 companies.

http://www.house.gov/ The House of Representatives is found here.

http://www.hwwilson.com/default.HTML Wilson Web replaces the print Wilson Library Bulletin.

http://www.law.cornell.edu/supct/supct.table.html Decisions of the United States Supreme Court is a database created from the Legal Information Institute at Cornell University Law School that has decisions from 1990 to present.

http://www.lib.umich.edu/libhome/ The University of Michigan Document Center provides full access to a variety of government documents, or go to **http://www.lib.umich.edu/libhome/ Documents.center/docnews.html** for the government documents that are generating news.

http://www.lib.utexas.edu/Libs/PCL/Map_collection/Map_ collection.html This is one of the most extensive map collections, from a street map of Jerusalem to a route through Yellowstone.

http://www.main.com/maptravel/ The International Map Trade Association will take you around the world as well as around the Web.

http://www.nasa.gov/ You can always explore NASA at this site.

http://www.newslink.org Newslink is one of the definitive sites to on-line publications with over six hundred newspapers and six hundred magazines available.

http://www.nih.gov/, the National Institutes of Health, or **http://www.nlm.nih.gov/**, the National Library of Medicine, are two spots that are better for surfing for health topics.

http://www.nmaa.si.edu National Museum of American Art Web site. The Smithsonian Institution Research Information System on Telnet is at **ssiris.si.edu** and is linked to the National Museum of American Art homepage.

http://www.nsf.gov/ Try the Web site of the National Science Foundation as a gateway to research facilities.

http://www.odci.gov This Central Intelligence Agency (CIA) Web site allows you to learn more about the CIA, review sources of agency publications, and search the public affairs information file with general background and public documents.

http://www.sec.gov Securities and Exchange Commission's Web site, EDGAR, allows anyone to tap into its colossal storehouse of corporate data for free.

http://www.si.edu The Smithsonian Institution estimates it would require at least twenty-five hours to download the output from the Smithsonian's sixteen museums and galleries in Washington and New York, from the National Zoo and from the National Gallery of Art. But what a boon for writers to be able to visit without ever leaving home!

http://www.si.sgi.com/organiza/affil/natgal/start.html is the National Gallery's Web site.

http://www.whitehouse.gov/ You can reach the White House at this site.

http://www-map.lib.umn.edu/ Need to know your way around college campuses? Try the Map Library at the University of Minnesota.

http://www-nmd.usgs.gov/www/html/ The U.S. Geological Survey provides continuously updated information about the planet.

lists@abii.com American Business Lists ONLINE® E-mail has mailing lists and contact information for over 11 million businesses in the U.S. and Canada; consumer lists that can target 84 million households; 11 million high school and college students; 500,000 + physicians and lawyers as well as car owners, insurance agents, investors, millionaires, fax numbers, public companies; and many other services.

Here are some sites that offer resources for writers:

- The *Editorial Eye* at **http://www.eei-alex.com/eye/**
- The National Writers Union at **http://www.nwu.org/nwu/**
- The Quill Society (for criticism) at **http://web.aimnet.com/ ~hyatt/quill/quilhome.html**
- Salon features articles on cultural issues at **http:// www.salon1999.com/**

Libraries throughout the world can be found on the Web's virtual library system of Virginia at **http://www.mcw.edu/lib/archive/ web-4lib/current/0006.html** where such databases as GPO Monthly, ArticleFirst, Applied Science & Technology, Biological Index and the Encyclopedia Britannica can be accessed.

Specialized library on-line systems include LEXIS/ NEXIS, which is the most heavily used commercial system in the library and technology fields. The database carries the full text of the *New York Times* plus thousands of legal, medical and general full-text information. NEXIS is the news side of the system; LEXIS offers a variety of full-text information on legal and regulatory materials.

WESTLAW is another full-text legal database that allows a novice to search easily by just typing in "find information about . . . ." The articles are listed in the order of word occurrence and word importance. It also offers the user a legal thesaurus and synonyms. A new addition to WESTLAW is LawTalk™, which is voice-activated from search through display. As the user speaks, the recognized words are displayed on the computer screen and can be adjusted for spelling so that the system will respond with correct information. LawTalk™ is also able to link up with WordPerfect word processing software so that a user can dictate letters, memos and legal documents.

DIALOG Information Systems provides easy access to full-text newspapers, magazines and directories from around the country. You can tap into *Dow Jones News/Retrieval*, the *Wall Street Journal* and *Barron's* to name just a few financial gateways that are available.

While you are doing your research, don't let your focus get too narrow. This is the same technique your amateur sleuth needs to use when you write a scene where they are using the Internet to get information on the case at hand. Have your sleuth compare what they've been told with the paper trail they are finding and look for inconsistencies. Remember, it's usually the trivial details that trip people up.

Information Brokers

If your sleuth gets a hot lead but doesn't know where or how to proceed, do what real-life private detectives do: Go to an information broker. Information brokers collect and sell data and are able to provide nationwide searches quickly and efficiently. Only a few database services deal with people on a case-by-case basis. But your sleuth should know that they can readily access the *PeopleTracker* database, which just about duplicates all the public records they might have to laboriously hunt through.

To find such information services, send your sleuth reaching for the yellow pages or send them back to the Internet at **http://www.investigator.com/bri**.

Disability Access

If your amateur sleuth or an associate has a disability, the information superhighway is still a viable resource. You can inform readers of how those with disabilities are able to use the Internet. For further information on how to make your writing accurate, contact the General Services Administration's Center for Information Technology Accommodation (CITA) on their Web home page at **http://www.gsa.gov/coca**. Here you'll find current information on legislation and issues, text of applicable laws, and a list of vendors selling computer accessibility products. Some technology companies post information on how their products can be used by the disabled. Apple Computer's is at **http://www.apple.com/disability/welcome.html**.

Most of the new computers allow the user to customize for disabilities. If your amateur is mobility, hearing or visually impaired, the computer can be made easier to use. Adjustments to the video display, mouse and/or keyboard settings, and the use of sound can help them navigate through computer programs. There's even a Braille monitor available for the blind plus text-to-speech synthesizers, voice-command software and touch-screen technology.

Some Internet Controversy

The following information is both a warning and a note of interest for possible plot usage. While you're busy combing the World Wide Web and other various sites on the Internet for facts and data, you won't be able to ignore the vast array of how-to pages. As we mentioned before, the probable to the improbable is out there.

After the explosion at the Federal Building in Oklahoma, it was reported that the formula for the bomb was available to one and all on the Internet. Law enforcement officials are expanding their efforts to catch up with the growing world of computer crime. The majority of computer misconduct is still hacking and money laundering, but criminals are increasing their use of computers for everything from making bomb threats to cyberpornography.

For the last two years, the FBI has been quite active in an undercover operation known as "Innocent Images," which investigates on-line pedophiles and child pornography sites. In September 1995, their work resulted in fifteen arrests and the searches of 125 suspects' computers. The FBI reports that they are getting as many as three complaints a day about on-line child pornography and messages seeking sex with minors. They do acknowledge, however, that this is a minute and difficult-to-find area among all the communication on the Internet and other commercial networks. Many of the on-line services offer parental control software so that children can be protected from the more graphic features in cyberspace.

On December 29, 1995, CompuServe bowed to pressure from German authorities and eliminated access to the more erotic and graphic Web sites for its four million customers worldwide. This has sent an alarm about future global censorship throughout the Internet and World Wide Web. As of January 2, 1996, Congress is still considering a telecommunications reform bill that would impose criminal penalties on people who make available to children "indecent" material over on-line services.

One of the most controversial aspects of the Internet is that you can do things on it that you'd get arrested for if you did them in person, over the phone or via the mail. Like other highways, the user takes a chance of picking up hitchhikers. There have been constant warnings about on-line dating and relationship services that can turn into computer stalking. As of October 1995, it became illegal in Connecticut (and is pending in other states) to threaten or harass someone using the Internet. If convicted, violators can be fined up to $500 and spend up to three months in prison. If the violator has a previous felony conviction, the punishment escalates to a $5,000 fine and five years in prison.

Enforcement of such a law is acknowledged to be a logistical nightmare, since the law is local and the offender may live in another state. Plus faking an identity or keeping yourself anonymous is so easy when a molester's MO becomes a modem.

Civil libertarians view the law as a desire to slow the flow of traffic on the information superhighway because, supposedly, it is nothing more than full of smut. As of December 1995, while the technology is available, there is no software that can tell who is accessing this or any information. Even when such technology becomes available, this will, no doubt, become a highly explosive legal issue. If a warrant is needed to search a person's phone records, a warrant will be needed to see who is downloading, via telephone lines, information off the Internet.

Viruses

Both you and your amateur sleuth need to be aware that computer systems can contract the dreaded electronic disease known as a computer virus. Viruses usually attach or insert themselves in a file or the boot sector of a disk. They are spread via shared floppy disks, networks or on-line services. Some viruses are harmless and just annoying; others can destroy or corrupt data and cause a system or program to malfunction. There are antivirus programs and hardware available to search out and isolate infected files and remove the virus from your computer's software.

Writer's Research Note

No one is immune. Even the United State's Military Defense System has been hit with a virus. But what a novel idea for a blackmail plot! "Give me millions or I will activate the virus that's been installed in your company's computer system."

Hackers

Your amateur sleuth can either learn to be a hacker or learn to foil one, which means you will have to know how to do both to write scenes credibly. Computer hacking, despite being a federal crime, is still going on. Leaving your computer modem on makes your sleuth vulnerable to a roving hacker out for entertainment.

Businesses, banks, colleges and universities have all been on the receiving end of being "hacked" into by anyone from students who want to change their grades to people who want to lower their utility bills or increase their bank accounts. There are quite a few how-to books that go into the techniques of hacking along with the jargon.

A Positive Note

The Internet has joined forces with the Missing and Exploited Children National Center in Arlington, Virginia. If you are writing a missing child theme in your mystery novel, you can have your amateur sleuth tap into their more than one thousand postings at **http://www.missingkids.org**. Here your detective will be able to access the same educational resources that are made available to law enforcement officials. Plus their two databases are open for your inspection. One, featuring the one thousand high-profile media cases, have original photos of children alongside those that have been aged by forensic artists. These artists use software from plastic surgeons and combine it with photos of the children to stretch facial images. The results are then merged with photos of other siblings or parents at the same age. The

---

Breaking and Entering on the Internet

- 500 percent increase in hacker break-ins since 1991.
- 20 percent of the companies using the Internet to exchange information had experienced successful *or* attempted break-ins.
- Twenty companies reported security-related losses exceeding one million dollars.
- Two-thirds of the companies encountered viruses.
- 40,000 computers with Internet access were attacked by hackers in 1994.
- Most companies admit they don't have the right software or expertise to foil hackers.

> *Source: Computer Emergency Response Team at Carnegie Mellon University and survey by Ernst & Young and* Information Week, *October, 1995.*

---

results are adjusted for wardrobe, hairstyle and color changes to give a new photo of what the child may look like now.

In a phone interview, Peter Banks of the Missing and Exploited Children National Center reported that they can have a missing child posted on their Web site in under two hours. And while fingerprints are nice, the single most valuable tool is a photo of the child. More than one million incidents of missing children are reported each year; 600,000 of them are recorded immediately by police in the NCIC computers. It is estimated that 347,000 are family abductions, but nearly 5,000 are stranger abductions, with over 300 of those resulting in long-term kidnappings and/or death.

For the past ten years, the Missing and Exploited Children National Center relied on photos being circulated nationwide on milk cartons or in a fifty-seven million card mass-mailing. One out of seven of the children pictured is recovered. Banks said the hope is to increase that number with the Internet Web site. There are currently six thousand active missing children cases in the U.S.

Using the Internet and the World Wide Web, you can access seemingly endless reference sources from around the

Take this challenge from Peter Banks at the Missing and Exploited Children Center:

1. Test your skills at being an amateur detective on-line.
2. Tap into their Web site.
3. Locate a missing child in your area.
4. See if you can put together a paper trail and find one of the missing children.

Their phone number is: 800-The Lost

Remember: If you find something, call them or the police or FBI. Don't attempt to apprehend!

world. That will make you and, indirectly, your amateur sleuth an expert on either a single topic or variety of topics.

As you can see, you can't overlook the information super-highway as a plot device. Whether or not you or your amateur sleuth is computer savvy, a whole new world of computer crime is at your fingertips.

Computers aren't just in the office. They are in our homes, cars and even our pockets. Technology is reaching out and into the world that the amateur inhabits. How author and sleuth use this advantage (and sometimes disadvantage) can make for an exceptionally rich story.

The more information you acquire, the more fertile your mind becomes. Sometimes you can extend fiction with technology. I (Elaine) did this in my two mystery novels featuring investigative reporter Nikki Holden: *Dangerous Places* and *Dark Corners*. The first novel featured interactive home gambling courtesy of a satellite. I "created" this idea in 1983 and have just learned that interactive home gambling is now on the Internet (yes, for money!).

My second novel, *Dark Corners* in 1988, used moving, full-size computer holographic images as a component of the story. This technology was available at the time in a limited, experimental form. In 1996, computerized, full-sized moving holographic images are being used by the military to train weapons units and fighter pilots.

How an Amateur Sleuth Can Use Technology

Today's amateur sleuth is surrounded by technology. They need to know how to use hardware technology correctly and effectively so they can ask the right questions to get answers that can help solve the case. In this chapter, we are going to show how you can use actual hardware instruments effectively as plot devices in your mystery novel.

Your amateur sleuth needs to be proficient in knowing how to get clues from the various equipment that is found in homes and offices. Here are some answers to a variety of questions on how to use hardware technology that will further help in the creation and education of both you and your amateur sleuth.

Telephone Technology

When Alexander Graham Bell invented the telephone in 1876, it was labeled a trend. In 1994, that trend accounted for 465 billion local calls, 59.7 billion long-distance calls and 23.8 billion in-state toll calls in the U.S. The telecommunications industry is holding its collective breath waiting to see if reform measures will be passed and change the face of the current seven regional Bell companies.

As of December 1995, the following companies service the U.S.:

NYNEX:	ME VT NH MA RI NY CT
Bell Atlantic:	NJ MD PA WV VA DE
Bell South:	NC KY SC GA FL AL MS LA TN
SBC Communications:	TX OK AR MO KS
Ameritech:	OH IN IL MI WI
Pacific Telesis:	HI CA NV
US West:	AK WA OR ID MT WY UT CO AZ ND SD NE IA MN

The telephone is more than just a base and receiver. Technology has gifted the actual transmission lines with an amazing collection of services that a smart sleuth must know about. What can telephone service provide? Just about anything if someone is willing to pay the price. Today, most residential and business phones have one or more of these add-ons:

Call Waiting
While you're talking, a beep or click alerts you that someone else is trying to reach you. If you don't want any interruptions while you're making a call, press *70 and anyone trying to call in will get a busy signal.

Three-Way Calling
This allows you to talk to two people at the same time without putting anyone on hold.

Voice Mail
Each person at the same phone number can have their own personal mailbox that answers calls and records messages when they're away or on the line.

Writer's Research Note

Maybe that alibi, "I was home talking on the phone" isn't as viable as it used to be. The home number that was called could have been forwarded anywhere!

Call Forwarding

This sends calls to another location. Now, no one ever has to know you're not home.

Personal Ring

This allows several different phone numbers to use one line but each number has a distinctive ring. The phone company allows each number its own phone book listing.

Priority Calls

You can assign a different ring to up to fifteen callers, without their knowledge, so that you know by sound who's on the other end of the line.

Easy Voice

You can actually dial the phone with your voice. The sound of *your* voice, or other members of your household or business, automatically dials up to fifty names on a preprogrammed phone list.

Repeat Dialing

Available as either a monthly fee or on individual calls with the code *66 to engage and *86 to disengage, repeat dialing automatically redials a number over and over then signals you that the number is available and places the call automatically.

Call Block

This monthly service automatically rejects calls from a specific list of phone numbers that you provide. The caller gets a recorded message, the user hears nothing. After a harassing phone call, you can dial *60 and follow the instructions. The caller's number will be blocked even if you don't know it.

Call Trace

A great feature that allows you to activate the feature on a per call basis by pressing *57, which forwards a record of the call to the phone company and police department. *This is evidence* they can use. One drawback: Call trace doesn't work if the caller is on a cellular phone.

Return Call

Did your amateur need to know who just called but didn't leave a message? Have them press *69 to activate (*89 to disengage) and they will hear the phone number of the person who called. Then they can either press #1 and be automatically connected or hang up. The service will also tell if it's an out-of-area or unlisted number. **Warning:** If this function is used to return annoyance calls, it *cannot be used as legal evidence if charges are brought.* The police advise against confronting crank callers because it may antagonize or encourage them. It's better to use Call Trace.

Writer's Research Note

Return call works on a per phone line basis, not per telephone. Have your sleuth check to see if there is more than one phone line coming into the house. If so, check each line.

Caller ID

Caller ID is one of the most popular and growing services that the phone company is providing. An ID box is attached to a phone and shows the number of the person who is calling. It also shows a log of who called while you were not home; deluxe ID's show each person's name as well as their number.

If you are the caller, you can prevent your number from being displayed on someone's ID box, at no charge, by dialing *67 before each call you place whether it's local or long distance. All that shows on the box is the letter *P.* If you do not choose that option, then your phone number, and possibly your name, will show up on an ID box even if it is an unlisted and/or unpublished number.

The caller ID subscriber also has the option to choose to reject calls from people who block their names and numbers by activating the Anonymous Call Reject (ACR) by dialing *77. The phone will not ring and callers will hear an announcement that their blocked calls are not being accepted. ACR is deactivated by dialing *87. Some of the phone companies are allowing people to unblock phone numbers on a per-call basis by dialing *82.

Caller ID went nationwide by order of the Federal Communications Commission on December 4, 1995. The ID display will now show the area code as well as the phone number. The FCC granted extensions to some of the smaller telephone companies that didn't have the needed equipment to offer this service and to California, which had imposed public education requirements that have not been met by any phone company in the state.

Pay telephones and party lines don't have to have the Caller ID equipment available until January 1, 1997. Businesses with 1-800 or 1-888 numbers have a system called "automatic number ID," which is similar to Caller ID and cannot be blocked.

Caller ID was initially believed to be used by the paranoid, but it has since become an invaluable communications tool that can work for or against you. The FCC has also barred companies that are gathering data through caller ID from selling information without the caller's permission.

Caller ID boxes are available for as little as thirty dollars. Some of the newer telephones come with ID boxes built right into communication phone packages for both home and office.

Making the Most of Telephone Hardware

Okay, so line service is smart. How does it help the amateur sleuth? Because today's telephone hardware is equally as smart.

The Redial Button

When your sleuth hits the redial button, it will put them in touch with the last person that was dialed from a particular

---

Writer's Research Note

All of this wonderful technology works both ways, so if you decide to have your amateur sleuth get harassing or obscene phone calls, have them call the phone company's Annoyance Phone Bureau. Or use this technology for your amateur sleuth to find out if the victim was on the receiving end of problem calls.

---

phone. If the phone has an LCD (liquid crystal display) or ID unit attached, the phone number becomes visible to the sleuthing eye. If no numeric display is evident, the tones themselves will determine what number was called. The clever amateur is likely to hit redial, wait for a response, then affect a clever ploy to extract the name of the person who answered. No response or display? Try tape recording the tones for future use in working on the number. *Remember*: Each telephone's redial button will show you who was called from that particular phone. So be smart and hit the redial button on *every* telephone, whether it's wired, cordless or cellular.

If no one answers and your detective can view the number, then use the reverse phone directory that's available at the public library to find out who is assigned that phone number. **Warning:** Redial is a limited function that may only work three times before being canceled. Your amateur could end up listening to just the dial tone.

The Auto Dial Feature

Have your sleuth check to see if the telephone has an auto dial feature. Often either the name or telephone number is listed on the directory card that is attached to the corresponding station key. When the station key is pressed, the number is automatically dialed. Again, if the phone has an LCD feature, the number will be visible. If there is not an LCD feature, you sleuth can match tones to gain the phone number and trace it back through the reverse telephone directory. Or they can try to acquire the person's name using a clever direct contact pretext.

Stored Numbers

On some large desk phones, what your detective sees isn't the only thing that's available. The more sophisticated the phone, the more information it contains.

Some models and phone/fax machines store numbers that go beyond the visible directory card. For example, if the card directory and station keys show twelve storage positions, try hitting auto dial and choose a number between 13 and 40 on the key pad. Then listen to see if a number is automatically dialed.

Then there's the boldly shown secret key. Your sleuth can try to see if a secret number has been programmed in by hitting auto dial then any two-digit number combination from 00 through 40 followed by the secret button.

Even luckier is the amateur sleuth who can find the manual that goes to some of today's more complicated phone systems.

Writer's Research Note

Can your amateur sleuth legally record a telephone conversation? Yes, says the Federal Communications Commission, as long as you let the other party know that you're recording. Beep tones are not necessary; just a verbal notification at the beginning of the conversation. Check your local regulations as they do vary despite the FCC rule.

Cordless Phones

Cordless phones allow your sleuth to talk and move around while investigating a room. The new digital spread-spectrum phones operate at 900 megahertz (MHz), which makes for less interference (better voice quality) because the phone isn't on the same frequency as microwave ovens and fluorescent lights. Spread-spectrum means the signal moves rapidly across the frequency range, reducing chances of it running into any other signal.

At least ten channels are needed because multiple channels allow switching so that overlapping conversations from other

---

Writer's Research Note

Only digital phones offer eavesdropping protection. Analog phones can easily have their conversations overheard on scanners or other telephones. If your sleuth lives in an apartment building, it is perfectly credible for them to overhear incriminating phone conversations while they are on an analog cordless phone ordering Chinese take-out.

---

cordless phones in the area (especially apartment houses) can be avoided. Most cordless phones have the same features as their deskmates.

Cellular Phones

When they have a cellular phone, your amateur sleuth never has to be out of reach or unable to call 911. Cellular phones first appeared in cars as rather heavy, cumbersome units that were left in the glove compartment. Now they have become pocket-sized and smaller. There is even a unit called a mastoid conductor that tucks neatly behind your ear and, coming in 1997, a wrist phone that connects to a watch and a pop-up handset.

Cellular phones are sophisticated two-way radios that get service from a matrix of transmitters or cell sites from around the world. Because of all the cell hopping, your transmission is subject to interference and signal loss when going through tunnels, mountains or even parking garages. Cellular phones with more powerful receivers are the best performers. Like their cordless cousins, digital calls can be scrambled to prevent eavesdropping but most cellular service is still analog.

Nearly all cellular phones share the following features:

Dual/Multiple NAM

Most phones will support more than one phone number assignment module (NAM), which means the same phone can have more than one number. *Remember*: Have your amateur sleuth check local service in cities where a suspect travels frequently to see if they have another phone number.

Paging

Certain cellular phones duplicate as a pager, allowing receipt of numeric and alphanumeric text messages.

Call Restrictions

This allows control over what services you are willing to subscribe to and pay for; for example, some cellular phones restrict long-distance calling.

Locking

This keeps others from using your phone by having a password or keypad locking.

Emergency Call

This overrides locking when a 911 emergency call is pressed.

Memory

Memory lets you store frequently called numbers and access them by pushing just one or two numbers.

Plus

There are dozens of other features, especially on high-end phones, that let you connect a modem, fax machine or other advanced calling features. *Remember*: Your amateur detective's cellular phone is only as good as its rechargeable, long-life battery.

Answer, Please

Depending on the model, some answering machines do more than simply record incoming messages. They can note the day, date and time of the incoming call, as well as record two-way conversations and allow special messages to be left for code retrieval.

Digital machines record on chips rather than tape, which means no more losing messages if your worn tape snaps. *Remember*: Check the outgoing message as well as the incoming. **Warning:** When you rewind on some machines, you automatically erase all messages!

Just the Fax

Once viewed as office-only equipment, fax machines are everywhere—in homes and in cars; there are even pocket-sized wireless fax machines that work with pagers and cellular phones plus ones built into handheld notepad computers. Some models include built-in answering machines, Caller ID and copying functions. Fax machines keep a smart amateur in touch with just about everyone. By using a clever pretext, your sleuth can have previous faxes retransmitted to their fax machine.

Fax Memo:

Of the 17,653 police departments in the U.S. only 7,000 of them have fax machines!

Most fax machines provide a help button that will print out instructions for sending a fax, a basic features list, how to access programmed numbers, how to use auto dial and how to print a journal report. The journal shows the last twenty or more transmissions and receptions to that particular fax machine and usually the phone/fax number that sent them. This can provide your sleuth with information about who a suspect has been in contact with.

Pagers

The first commercial paging started in 1949. Back then the units received voices and, when people called the service company to have someone paged, their operators would broadcast their names to all paging units in the area. Like a CB-radio, you listened for your messages and ignored everyone else's. (Is there a retro mystery novel in that or what?)

Then came the beeper, where service companies could target their signal to your beeper and yours alone. Later, units went digital so you could view the number you were supposed to call. Ten years ago, letters were added so you could receive simple messages.

Today, there are over thirty million pagers in use in the

U.S. and that number increases daily. No longer the exclusive device of doctors and emergency workers, people such as school children, corporate officers and drug dealers are toting around a dazzling assortment of designer pagers, some so small they're embedded in watches and pens.

Pager technology is also evolving on a rapid scale. Once all that they noted were alphanumeric numbers; now some are set up to receive stock quotes, sports scores, messages from PC's and E-mail delivery. Pager technology may overtake the cellular phone as the remote communications choice. What's currently available for your amateur sleuth to use as a tool or to find as a clue and access information?

Two-Way Paging

Two-way paging allows your amateur to receive and respond to messages directly from a paging unit. SkyTel (1-800-759-8737) is the first company to offer this service. The pager weighs about 5.5 ounces and has a four-line, twenty-character LCD display. It receives text messages of up to five hundred characters that you can respond to immediately by choosing from a list of precomposed responses. If your sleuth has a palmtop computer, they can use a cable connection to the pager and compose their own response to zap off.

Voice Paging

This is a combination portable answering machine and pager. PageNet (1-800-724-3638) offers this service. Callers use an 800 number to leave a voice message, which is then transmitted to a paging unit. Instead of leaving the usual alphanumeric text, the pager stores up to four minutes of voice messages that can be played back.

Companies will soon be offering combination two-way voice paging. This will allow a person to reply to voice messages directly by speaking into the paging unit.

PC and Software Pagers

If your sleuth owns a notebook computer, their pager can interface directly with a PC and receive not only alphanumeric pages, but binary files as well, much like downloading information from the Internet.

More Added Pager Attractions

Mobytel (1-800-662-9835) offers a nationwide system that sounds like it came out of a science fiction novel:

- MobyTrac allows you to visually see the location of a vehicle in over 7,500 cities and towns across the U.S. using their satellite-based unit.

- MobyAlarm instantly connects you to a security firm if your vehicle is stolen, and both of you can track it.

- MobyMail gives E-mail and file transfer options.

- MobyFax lets you type @*fax* plus the phone number of any fax machine in the world and the fax is sent off.

- Plus—yes, there's more—it can remotely control door locks and other security devices.

- And, even after being turned off for weeks, all your messages are immediately available.

The typical pager fits neatly into a shirt pocket or purse. A tone or vibrator signals an incoming message, which is displayed on an easy-to-read LCD screen. Most have six to sixteen messages memory with a lock button to protect the numbers you want to save along with a time-and-day stamp of when the message was received by the paging unit. *Remember*: Have your amateur sleuth check phone numbers stored in the pager's memory. Those may be the last calls a victim received. **Warning:** Most school districts have forbidden students to carry pagers because of their popularity among drug dealers. The price is suspension.

More Gadgets Galore

Welcome to the world of adult toys. They aren't just for big boys either. Some of these items can be used by your amateur sleuth or be found by them as a clue.

Data Banks

Why have your detective find a note, when you can have them find a Data Bank? Data Banks can be as simple as holding just thirty names and telephone numbers (sort of a replacement for the little black book), or as complex as having 2K memory and being able to download into your home or office PC.

Data Banks store names, numbers, addresses and memos. They usually come equipped with an alarm, calculator, display clock, calendar and security code function. The how-to-use-it information can be found printed on the inside of the cover or in a mini-manual.

PDAs

Give your sleuth a PDA (personal digital assistant) or make them find one. These tiny, handheld machines organize and communicate with your bigger PC and other people. The PDA is what the open-road amateur or suspect can use to telephone or fax, collect E-mail messages, or make notes using a stylus on a touch screen, all while they're wandering around in search of clues.

Voicemates

These tiny memo-minders record for up to ninety seconds; some are capable of holding names and phone numbers. They can usually be found in a pocket, purse or clipped to an auto visor.

Television

"Television has brought back murder into the home—where it belongs." The late filmmaker, Alfred Hitchcock, made that statement in 1965 when he was interviewed by the London *Observer.* It's certainly a more powerful and truthful review than ones levied by most critics who have called television a "vast wasteland full of mindless images" (sounds like the review of the Internet!). And Hitchcock spoke the truth: Murder is back in the home via the evening news or courtesy of a movie.

The television set can be a powerful learning tool that can be used to increase your knowledge on various subjects as well as increase your creativity. Here you can put your senses to work, taking full advantage of the mannerisms and nuances of people of all ages, either sex and all ethnic backgrounds. This can prove to be that extra edge in creating a credible, realistic and memorable character—in this case, an amateur detective.

Your smart amateur detective knows enough to pop on the TV set. The television can provide information on a variety of topics that are of interest to the sleuth or facts on the crime at hand. The eye of the TV camera can be another visual aid, scanning the crime scene and the ensuing curious crowd. The reporter may be interviewing police officials or the onlookers, which will bring in new facts, either true or false, that may provide a clue. If the amateur sleuth happens to be a TV or newspaper reporter, this makes their continued interaction with crime logical and sets up credible mechanisms for the author.

Writer's Research Note

The media—TV, radio and print—is a powerful tool that can be *used, misused* and *manipulated.* One thing that the media and authorities do agree on is the power of the press. For example, 41 percent of missing children are found through media efforts.

Miscellaneous Gadgets

Other standard gadgets that have become necessities in the area of sleuthing include: voice-activated microcassette recorders— your amateur can either hide one in a room to catch conversations or find one that's been hidden; palm-size camcorders that are easy to conceal inside a book or between the branches of a potted palm, and can be fitted with infrared motion-recording activation devices; and regular cameras and videotape machines.

Counter-Spying

The more gadgets, the more spying. It always helps for an amateur sleuth to be slightly paranoid when the "game's afoot for real." So what's out there for you to help make your amateur sleuth, villain and mystery novel credible?

The 1995 holiday catalogue of a national chain of electronics stores offered fifteen different models of scanning radio receivers. While mostly purchased by police-band buffs and amateur radio operators, these scanners offer your sleuth (or your villain) a direct line to listen in on business and personal conversations on cordless and cellular phones.

The back pages of various electronics magazines show how inexpensive it is to order a microchip transmitter that, when placed inside a telephone, allows a person to hear *all* the conversations going on in a room, not just the ones coming over the phone lines.

There are over one hundred specialty spy stores in the United States selling equipment that a mere dozen years ago was available only to law enforcement officials. This includes pens and calculators that have built-in transmitters, telephone intercept units that are undetectable, and fax interceptors that can intercept a fax from any fax machine.

The same technology that has created the above gadgets allows anyone, professional or amateur, the ability to intercept communication. Telephones, faxes and computers are indispensable to businesses as well as the home. Yet new eavesdropping technology makes it easy for business competitors, disgruntled employees or vindictive personal acquaintances to become saboteurs.

There are ways to make your sleuth less vulnerable despite their owning state-of-the-art equipment.

Cordless and Cellular Phones

A snoop with a radio scanner can easily find and lock onto any individual phone and eavesdrop. While digital phones make it more difficult, your amateur's best option is to simply not discuss confidential matters on cordless and cellular phones.

Telephone Listening Devices

This chip is about the size of an ant and is installed inside the telephone, where it will pick up all phone and room conversations. These chips can be purchased in any electronics specialty store as can the components for more elaborate listening devices.

Fax Machines

Fax transmissions use the same telephone lines as voice communications, so they are equally susceptible to piracy. A fax machine is also a prime sight for placing an electronic bug.

Writer's Research Note

"Bug detectors" should be able to find these devices. But just like real insects, electronic wizards are able to evolve bugs that are immune to various detectors and, despite claims, no one detector can locate all types of bugs. Make sure your amateur sleuth looks for more than one type of bug.

Phone Wires

Remember, there are miles of wires running through office buildings and homes.Wiretapping is illegal without a warrant, but the person doing the tapping is usually going after illegal information and really doesn't care.

One place to have your amateur detective inspect for wiretaps is an office building's telephone switching room where the PBX (private branch exchange) system is housed. Contained here is a maze of colorful wires that connects all the phones, faxes and modems to the inside and outside world. The switching rooms are easily accessible, rarely locked or equipped with alarms so that anyone can get in and tap the lines.

Most PBX's are computer driven, meaning the intruder-hacker can manipulate software to create "softaps," the latest rage in telephone eavesdropping. The calls are routed to additional phones, which strip away privacy and any antieavesdropping measures that were taken. On most business phone systems, software tinkering may activate the telephone's microphone turning it into an all-purpose room bug even when the phone isn't being used.

How to conquer this situation? Your amateur sleuth can own a secure phone or suggest one for a colleague who's been having problems.

Technology and information can work for you as long as you know the correct way to have your amateur sleuth (or villain) use it as you plot your novel. The smart amateur sleuth needs to look at the big picture that encompasses not only equipment but the human element. All the secure technological devices in the world aren't worth much if the source of the problem is a human being.

The following chapters will provide you with information on how you can use the legal system to aid or hinder your amateur sleuth.

GUNS AND ARREST: WHAT THE AMATEUR CAN DO—LEGALLY

What can your amateur detective use to defend himself or herself or someone else? How can he or she make an arrest, or is that possible? There is a body of popular belief that says there is no such thing as citizen's arrest powers; there is another body of popular belief that says that citizen's arrest powers are extremely far-reaching. Like most popular beliefs, both of these are partly true and partly false. This chapter will examine the legalities of these matters, pointing out what is and is not appropriate in various jurisdictions.

Always remember these two things:

(1) Your fictional detective may do something whether it is legal or not; and

(2) Your fictional detective may get away with whatever he or she does whether it is legal or not.

You decide what happens on the basis of the law and the needs of your story. It is important to know the rules, and be consistent

---

Common Law vs. Statute Law

What is the difference between common and statute law?

Common law is the received body of traditional understandings, in many cases centuries old, that things are or are not to be done. In sociological terms, common law is a set of folkways. In general, most parts of common law have by now been either abandoned or codified.

Statute law is codified law, the body of laws that govern any political jurisdiction. In sociological terms, they would be considered mores.

In this book, the only common or statute laws to be addressed are criminal law and arrest and firearms law.

---

in breaking or not breaking them and seeing to it that appropriate consequences follow.

But both you and your amateur detective must keep in mind one important truth: Anyone who makes an arrest had better be prepared to back it up. Disregarding this rule can be a good way to get your character into deep guano. And disregarding this rule in real life can be a good way to get yourself killed. This book is intended to give advice to writers, not to would-be detectives.

You Have to Know the Rules in Order to Break Them Intelligently

Which brings us back to the points to be addressed in this chapter: May your amateur make a legal arrest in the location where your book is set? What may your amateur use for self-defense? People prowling around trying to solve mysteries are likely once in a while to find themselves in big trouble from an outraged witness or suspect, and this kind of trouble creates a good bit of the tension on which your story rides. Does your state law allow the carrying of firearms by public citizens? If so, must they be concealed, must they be visible, or may they be carried either way? Does your state allow the use of Mace or pepper spray?

To get the answers to these and other questions, we

Citizen's Arrest

In the states that have a statutory provision for citizen's arrest, the wording is almost always some variant of the following:

(1) A private person may arrest another without a warrant if:

(i) A felony has in fact been committed, and the arresting person has probable cause to believe that the person to be arrested committed it, or

(ii) The person to be arrested committed an offense, other than a felony, in the presence of the arresting person.

Therefore, we'll note standard wording for each state that uses it, and include under each state only unusual variants or additional information.

questioned the state attorneys general of all fifty states, U.S. and its possessions and territories, the Canadian attorney general, and the law library of the University of Utah. The answers here are as current as possible, but again, be aware that jurisdictions always change their laws and some counties and cities may have their own laws that supplement or even supplant state laws. So if possible, check for *local current* law unless you want to take a chance. And do notice that some state attorneys general are located in the largest city of the state rather than, or as well as, the state capitol.

Where do you go to check on laws? Some state attorneys general are more helpful than others. But at least the attorney general's office of your state can tell you where to find a law library to look things up for yourself. Intimidating though they might look, law books are actually pretty user-friendly, at least with the help of your closest law librarian. They tend to be well indexed and, if you carry along a small legal dictionary, you shouldn't run into any serious problems. Unless you're looking up barratry.

And now, a few definitions:

- *Felony*: Under English common law, on which laws of all of the United States other than Louisiana are based

Barratry

What is barratry, and why is it likely to give me trouble? It all depends on who you ask and on the location of the area you're researching.

In some codes, barratry is crime on the high seas. In other codes, it is stirring up unnecessary litigation. Be sure you know which you mean. And be sure your reader knows.

(Louisiana's law is based partly on the Napoleonic Code), a felony is a major crime. This is usually defined as a crime punishable by more than a year and a day of imprisonment and/or a fine of less than $10,000. But check your jurisdiction for its specific definition.

- *Misdemeanor*: Usually a crime punishable by less than a year and a day of imprisonment and/or a fine of less than $10,000. Again, check your jurisdiction for its specific definition.

- *Probable Cause*: Sufficient information to cause a reasonable person to think it likely that the situation is as it has been represented. For a private citizen to have probable cause to make an arrest, she must normally have personally seen the crime, know that a warrant for the crime exists, or have been told by a person whom she has reason to trust that this crime was committed and that this is the person who committed it.

- *Sufficient Cause*: See Probable Cause.

Mace and Other Noxious Sprays

This one we can answer in a hurry. As of the writing of this book, American sellers of self-defense sprays were mentioning in their advertisements that pepper spray (which comes in several brands) cannot be shipped outside of the United States except to Germany and to APO and FPO addresses. It cannot be shipped to California or Michigan at all, and it cannot be shipped to anyone who is not a law enforcement officer in Hawaii,

Rhode Island, New Jersey, Massachusetts, New York or in Baltimore and Annapolis, Maryland. Mace—this is a brand name, so don't talk about Pepper Mace unless you mean the brand of mixed pepper spray and Mace that is sold by the Mace manufacturer—cannot be shipped out of the United States except to Germany and to APO and FPO addresses. It cannot be sold at all in Hawaii, Rhode Island, New Jersey or Massachusetts, and it cannot be sold except to law enforcement officers in Baltimore and Annapolis, Maryland.

But always keep in mind that the fact that something is illegal in a given jurisdiction does not mean that your brilliant amateur, or your amateur's opposition, cannot have it and use it. Smuggling of weapons of all kinds is extremely prevalent, and we will mention it again as we go along.

One reiterated warning: The firearms laws we quote below are as current as we can make them *now*. But, as always, ask anyway. As criminal firepower expands, more and more states are making it legal for citizens to carry firearms in self-defense. As of this writing, nine states have passed CCW (carrying concealed weapons) laws in the last two years (1994-1995), and four more are expected to do so in 1996. A CCW law, or the lack of one, can be used to set your detective up for victory or for temporary defeat. Learn the rules and then work with them in your writing, or learn the rules and break them in your writing. You can do either one. But whichever you choose will affect your character's life.

What the Law Allows: United States of America

The federal Brady Law now takes precedence over state and local firearms laws *unless* the state in question already has laws in place which are equivalent to, or stricter than, the federal law. See the sidebar on page 122 for a summary of the Brady Law, a federal firearms act named for President Ronald Reagan's press secretary, who was permanently handicapped by the same would-be assassin who shot President Reagan.

Attorney General of **Alabama**
Alabama State House
11 South Union Street
Montgomery, AL 36130
(334) 242-7300

Citizen's Arrest
Rules of Alabama Supreme Court:
Rule 4.1. Arrest without a warrant.
(b) ARREST BY A PRIVATE PERSON.
[standard wording in Part (1)—see sidebar page 118]
(2) A private person making an arrest shall inform the person arrested of the cause of the arrest, except when such person is arrested in the actual commission of the crime or doing pursuit immediately thereafter. A private person making an arrest shall deliver the person arrested without unnecessary delay to a judge, magistrate, or law enforcement officer. If the person arrested is taken to a law enforcement officer, the officer shall proceed as provided in Rule 4.3(a).

Carrying a Weapon
Alabama must comply with the rules of the federal Brady Law. From Criminal Code of the State of Alabama:
13A-11-75. License to carry pistol in vehicle or concealed on person — Issuance; term; form; fee; revocation.
The sheriff of a county may, upon the application of any person residing in that county, issue a qualified or unlimited license to such person to carry a pistol in a vehicle or concealed on or about his person within this state for not more than one year from date of issue, if it appears that the applicant has good reason to fear injury to his person or property or has any other proper reason for carrying a pistol, and that he is a suitable person to be so licensed. The license shall be in triplicate, in form to be prescribed by the Secretary of State, and shall bear the name, address, description and signature of the licensee and the reason given for desiring a license. The original thereof shall be delivered to the licensee, the duplicate shall, within seven days, be sent by registered or certified mail to the Director of

The Brady Law

The Brady Law covers handguns, requires a five-business-day waiting period, and makes the chief law enforcement officer in the place where the purchaser resides responsible for making a criminal record check. It requires the following identification questions to be answered: name, address, date of birth and driver's license check, and makes the Social Security number, height, weight, sex and place of birth optional.

The Brady Law provides these disqualifications: A person may not purchase a firearm if he is convicted of or under indictment for any crime punishable by imprisonment for over one year, has any record of substance abuse, has been adjudicated mentally defective or committed to a mental institution, is an illegal alien, if he has renounced citizenship, or if he has been dishonorably discharged from the United States armed forces.

Public Safety, and the triplicate shall be preserved for six years by the authority issuing the same.

Note that all this applies to carrying a *concealed* weapon. A state ruling on March 22, 1984, provides that a person otherwise allowed to own or borrow a pistol (see below) may carry an *unconcealed* weapon at any time when he is on foot, unless he is in a place where pistols are not allowed to anyone except law enforcement officials on duty, and no one without a permit is allowed to carry a pistol in a vehicle.

Summing up the rest of the Alabama code, it is made clear that a pistol permit may be issued *only* by the sheriff of the county the applicant lives in; that no person "who has been convicted of committing or attempting to commit a crime of violence" may own a pistol or have one under his control; and that a pistol may not be delivered in any way (selling or lending) to a person under the age of eighteen or to one who has been convicted of a crime of violence, is a drug addict, an alcoholic, or "a person of unsound mind."

Attorney General of **Alaska**
P.O. Box K, State Capitol
Juneau, AK 99811-0300
(907) 465-3600

Citizen's Arrest
[standard wording]

Carrying a Weapon
Alaska must comply with the rules of the federal Brady Law. In general, Alaska prohibits full automatic weapons; rifles with barrels shorter than sixteen inches; shotguns with barrels shorter than eighteen inches; and rifles, shotguns and over-under or side-by-side rifle-shotgun combinations with an overall length shorter than twenty-six inches.

The only person not permitted to own a weapon in Alaska is a convicted felon.

Alaska issues permits [Title 11, Chapter 46, Article 1: 18.65.700. a.] "to carry a concealed handgun to a person who

(1) applies in person at an office of the Alaska State Troopers;

(2) qualifies under AS 18.65.705;

(3) submits a completed application on a form provided by the department . . .

(4) submits two complete sets of fingerprints . . .

(5) submits evidence of competence with handguns. . . ."

Alaska is probably in the process, as this book is written, of rewriting its laws to conform to the Brady Law; however, there is a problem in Alaska because of its immense wilderness area and the high percentage of people who live partly or totally off the land. A strict firearms law is almost totally unenforceable in Alaska.

Attorney General of **Arizona**
1275 West Washington Street
Phoenix, AZ 85007
(602) 542-4266

Citizen's Arrest
[standard wording]

Carrying a Weapon
Arizona must comply with the rules of the federal Brady Law. At present its laws regarding prohibited weapons are almost identical to those of Alaska. It prohibits the following persons from owning weapons: a person likely to constitute a danger to himself/herself or to others, a person convicted of a violent felony, or a person in jail or prison.

A permit to carry a concealed weapon cannot be made until after training requirements have been met. The person must then contact the Department of Public Safety for exact requirements to be met.

Attorney General of **Arkansas**
200 Tower Building
4th and Center Streets
Little Rock, AR 72201
(501) 682-2007

Citizen's Arrest
Arkansas appears not to have any laws for or against citizen's arrest, except for shoplifting arrests by a merchant. Let your amateur use his or her own judgment, and be prepared to back it up.

Carrying a Weapon
Arkansas must comply with the rules of the federal Brady Law. At present Arkansas forbids only the following weapons: machine guns, sawed-off shotguns and weapons with silencers. The following people are prohibited from owning weapons: convicted felons, mentally defective persons and persons involuntarily committed to mental institutions.

Arkansas permits the carrying of concealed firearms under fairly lenient rules. Check with the chief law enforcement officer—sheriff or police chief—in the area you're setting your story.

Attorney General of **California**
1515 K Street, Suite 511
Sacramento, CA 95814
(916) 324-5437

Citizen's Arrest
[standard wording]

Carrying a Weapon
California has met or exceeded the standards of the federal Brady Law and, therefore, is not required to comply with the federal law. California's firearms laws are among the most complicated in the United States. Any one of a very long list of crimes and other conditions will prohibit a California resident from possessing any firearms, and no one may purchase a firearm who has not completed a firearms safety course and obtained a permit for purchase. A concealed weapon normally may be carried only within a motor vehicle trunk or otherwise in a locked container, or carried "by the person directly to or from any motor vehicle for any lawful purpose and, while carrying the firearm, the firearm is contained within a locked container" (12026.1 [2]). A civilian is not permitted to carry a concealed weapon on his or her person under any circumstances.

California law also requires that all firearms dealers put up a conspicuous sign with this message: "IF YOU LEAVE A LOADED FIREARM WHERE A CHILD OBTAINS AND IMPROPERLY USES IT, YOU MAY BE FINED OR SENT TO PRISON."

Under the provisions of the Roberti-Roos Assault Weapons Control Act of 1989, all designated assault weapons are prohibited from sale.

Attorney General of **Colorado**
1525 Sherman Street
Denver, CO 80203
(303) 866-3052

Pistols vs. Revolvers

What's the difference between a pistol and a revolver?

A revolver is often referred to as a pistol, but technically the term "pistol" refers to an automatic or semiautomatic firearm with a barrel length shorter than twelve inches. See Writer's Digest Books *Armed and Dangerous* and *Scene of the Crime* for more information.

Citizen's Arrest

Colorado appears not to have any laws for or against citizen's arrest. Let your amateur use his or her own judgment, and be prepared to back it up.

Carrying a Weapon

Colorado has met or exceeded the standards set by the federal Brady Law and, therefore, is not required to comply with the federal law.

Colorado prohibits sale of weapons to persons convicted of felonies or certain misdemeanors. It does not permit civilians to carry concealed weapons.

Attorney General of **Connecticut**
55 Elm Street
Hartford, CT 06106
(203) 566-2026

Citizen's Arrest

Connecticut appears not to have any laws for or against citizen's arrest, except for shoplifting arrests by a merchant. Let your amateur use his or her own judgment, and be prepared to back it up.

Carrying a Weapon

Connecticut has met or exceeded the standards of the federal Brady Law and, therefore, is not required to comply with the federal law.

The firearms laws of Connecticut, Title 29 of the state code, are particularly complex in wording. Summed up, they state that (1) a person who is legally authorized to carry a firearm in any other state may receive a permit to carry a concealed weapon within any township, borough or county in Connecticut; (2) an application for a pistol permit by a resident of Connecticut requires completion of an approved course in firearms safety, no record of mental illness within the last twenty years, not being under a restraining order involving use of physical force, and not being an illegal alien; and (3) no one may purchase a pistol or revolver without first obtaining a permit to carry one.

Attorney General of **Delaware**
820 North French Street
Dover, DE 19801
(302) 577-3838

Citizen's Arrest
Delaware appears not to have any laws for or against citizen's arrest, except for shoplifting arrests by a merchant. Let your amateur use his or her own judgment, and be prepared to back it up.

Carrying a Weapon
Delaware has met or exceeded the standards of the federal Brady Law and, therefore, is not required to comply with the federal law.

It has a rather lengthy classification of people not permitted to own firearms. It does not permit the carrying of concealed weapons by civilians.

Corporation Counsel of the **District of Columbia**
441 4th Street N.W.
Washington, DC 20001
(202) 727-6248

Citizen's Arrest
We were unable to find any information about citizen's arrest in the District of Columbia. However, it is safe to say that attempting such an arrest, whether it is legal or illegal, is unsafe.

Carrying a Weapon
The District of Columbia, as it is federally governed, complies with the rules of the federal Brady Law. It (1) registers "all firearms owned by private citizens"; (2) limits "the types of weapons persons may lawfully possess"; (3) purportedly assures "that only qualified persons are allowed to possess firearms"; and (4) makes "it more difficult for firearms, destructive devices, and ammunition to move in illicit commerce within the District of Columbia" [DC Code ann. 6-2301]. (Anybody who watches television news or reads newspapers or news magazines realizes the last clause is a sick joke; firearms smuggling into the District of Columbia and criminal use of firearms there are extremely prevalent.) It does not permit the carrying of concealed weapons by civilians.

Office of the Attorney General of **Florida**
Department of Legal Affairs
The Capitol
Tallahassee, FL 32399-1050
(904) 487-1963

Citizen's Arrest
Florida appears not to have any laws for or against citizen's arrest, except for shoplifting arrests by a merchant. Let your amateur use his or her own judgment, and be prepared to back it up.

Carrying a Weapon
Florida has met or exceeded the standards of the federal Brady Law and, therefore, is not required to comply with the federal law.

Keep an eye on this section; Florida's firearms laws tend to change rapidly. At present, according to **F.S. 1993, 790.06,** a license to carry a concealed weapon may be issued to a U.S. resident or a foreign consular official, provided the person is twenty-one or older, "does not suffer from a physical infirmity which prevents the safe handling of a weapon or firearm"; has not been convicted of a felony or a violent misdemeanor, does not have a record of substance abuse including alcohol, has completed a firearms safety course, and has "not been adjudicated an incapacitated person" or "committed to a mental institution. . . ." The applicant must provide complete identification along with evidence that he or she meets all the requirements listed, a complete set of fingerprints and a good photograph. Even with the permit, there is a long list of places such as schools, courtrooms and police stations in which a firearm may not be carried.

Attorney General of **Georgia**
132 State Judicial Building
Atlanta, GA 30334
(404) 656-4585

Citizen's Arrest
Georgia Code 17-4-60. Grounds for arrest.
[standard wording]
Additional information:
If the offense is a felony and the offender is escaping or attempting to escape, a private person may arrest him upon reasonable and probable grounds of suspicion.
According to Johnson v. Jackson, 140 Ga. App. 252,230 S.E.2d 756 (1976), "A private man has quite as much power to arrest a fugitive felon, where the emergency calls for immediate action, as a public officer, and while doing so, is equally under the protection of the law."
A private citizen making an arrest must deliver the arrestee to a police officer or magistrate immediately. However, a police officer making an arrest may take up to a maximum of forty-eight hours to deliver the offender before a judicial officer to obtain a warrant, if none exists, or for arraignment if a warrant does exist.

Carrying a Weapon

Georgia must comply with the rules of the federal Brady Law; however, the federal five-day waiting period does not apply to persons with valid permits/licenses to carry handguns issued within the past five years.

According to **Ga. 16-11-129**, a person may be granted a license to carry a concealed firearm if he or she is over twenty-one years of age; is not a fugitive from justice or under indictment; has not been convicted of a felony or violent misdemeanor; has not been treated for substance abuse; and has not been convicted of "unlawful manufacture, distribution, possession, or use of a controlled substance or other dangerous drug." The applicant must be fingerprinted and a record check must be made.

Attorney General of **Hawaii**
425 Queen Street
Honolulu, HI 96813
(808) 586-1282

Citizen's Arrest

Hawaii law provides that anyone "in the act of committing a crime may be arrested by any person present, without a warrant" (Bassiouni 88).

Carrying a Weapon

Hawaii has met or exceeded the standards of the federal Brady Law and, therefore, is not required to comply with the federal law.

Hawaii prohibits even the acquisition of a firearm without a permit, and the regulations for the permit, lengthy and strict, require completion of both a hunter education course and a firearms safety or training course. Further, any person who owns a weapon that he or she will take to Hawaii is required to "register the firearm within three days after arrival of the person or of the firearm, whichever arrives later" (134.3.a.) Private citizens are not permitted to carry concealed firearms.

Office of the Attorney General of **Idaho**
Statehouse, Room 210
P.O. Box 83720
Boise, ID 83720-0010
(208) 334-2400

Citizen's Arrest
Idaho law provides for citizen's arrest.
19-604. When private person may arrest.
[Parts 1 and 2 are standard wording.]
3. When a felony has been in fact committed, and he has reasonable cause for believing the person arrested to have committed it.
19-605. Magistrate may order arrest.—A magistrate may orally order a peace officer or private person to arrest any one committing or attempting to commit a public offense in the presence of such magistrate.

The law further provides that anybody who is making, or attempting to make, an arrest may ask for help from as many people as he considers necessary to make the arrest; however, he may use no more than reasonable force. For a felony, anyone making an arrest—even a private citizen—"may break open the door or window of the house in which the person to be arrested is, or in which there is reasonable ground for believing him to be, after having demanded admittance and explained the purpose for which admittance is desired" (**19-610** and **19-611**). The citizen making the arrest *may* then seize all weapons on the arrestee's person and *must* deliver them and the person arrested to a magistrate or to a police officer as soon as possible (**19-613** and **19-614**). This law is very unusual, and you might be able to use it effectively in fiction. (Speaking as a former police officer, I would very strongly *not* suggest actually doing this. If you use it in fiction, it will probably get your character in quite a lot of trouble, which may strengthen your plot.)

Carrying a Weapon
Idaho has met or exceeded the standards of the federal Brady Law and, therefore, is not required to comply with the federal law. A person wanting a license to carry a concealed

weapon must have been a resident of the state for at least ninety days. **18-3302** then states that the "citizen's constitutional right to bear arms shall not be denied to him, unless he:

(a) Is ineligible to own, possess or receive a firearm under the provisions of state or federal law; or"

—to sum up—has been convicted of, or is under indictment for, a felony or a violent misdemeanor; "is a fugitive from justice"; has a history of substance abuse; is mentally incapacitated; or has been dishonorably discharged from the armed forces. The applicant must provide considerable identification including proof of having completed a firearms training course, along with fingerprints for a records search. However, if there is substantial risk in delay, a person may be issued an emergency license while the complete application is being processed.

Office of the Attorney General of **Illinois**
500 South Second Street
Springfield, IL 62706
(217) 782-1090
(Note: The Attorney General of Illinois also has an office at 100 West Randolph Street, Chicago, IL 60601.)

Citizen's Arrest
[standard wording]

Carrying a Weapon
Illinois has met or exceeded the standards of the federal Brady Law and, therefore, is not required to comply with the federal law. Illinois requires a firearm owner's identification card, which will be issued only for good reason and to well-qualified people: no convicts, substance abusers, mentally ill or mentally retarded persons need apply. Illinois has reciprocity with Iowa, Missouri, Indiana, Wisconsin and Kentucky on firearm owner's identification cards. No civilian may carry a gun anywhere inside city limits except on his own land or in his own abode or fixed place of business. No civilian may carry a concealed firearm.

Office of the Attorney General of **Indiana**
Indiana Government Center South, Fifth Floor
402 West Washington Street
Indianapolis, IN 46204-2770
(317) 232-6201

Citizen's Arrest
Criminal Code Sec. 35-2.1-2.3(15)
The arrest of a person may be made lawfully . . . by . . .
a private citizen without a warrant upon reasonable information
that the accused stands charged in another state with a crime
punishable by death or imprisonment for a term exceeding one
year; but when so arrested the accused must be taken before a
judge or magistrate with all practicable speed and complaint
must be made against him under oath setting forth the ground
for the arrest as in the last section and his answer shall be heard
as if he had been arrested on warrant.

Carrying a Weapon
Indiana has met or exceeded the standards of the federal
Brady Law and, therefore, is not required to comply with the
federal law.
**Indiana Constitution, Article I, Section 32. [Right to bear
arms].** The people shall have a right to bear arms, for the defense
of them and the State.
Carrying a concealed weapon is permitted in Indiana.

Office of the Attorney General of **Iowa**
Hoover Building, Second Floor
Des Moines, IA 50319
(515) 281-3053

Citizen's Arrest
[standard wording]

Carrying a Weapon
Iowa has met or exceeded the standards of the federal
Brady Law and, therefore, is not required to comply with the

federal law. Iowa requires any person who wants to purchase a pistol or revolver to obtain an annual permit. During the time covered by the permit, the person may acquire one or more weapons. The permit may not be issued to a felon, a person under twenty-one without parental permission, or an "otherwise disqualified person" (724.19).

Carrying a concealed weapon is not permitted in Iowa.

Office of the Attorney General of **Kansas**
301 S.W. 10th Avenue
Topeka, KS 66612-1597
(913) 296-2215

Citizen's Arrest
22-2403. Arrest by private person. A person who is not a law enforcement officer may arrest another person when:

[Part (1) is standard wording.]

(2) any crime, other than a traffic infraction, has been or is being committed by the arrested person in view of the person making the arrest.

Carrying a Weapon
Kansas must comply with the rules of the federal Brady Law. Except for law enforcement officers, security guards and so forth, it is illegal to carry "any pistol, revolver or other firearm concealed on one's person except when on the person's land or in the person's abode or fixed place of business . . ." (**21-4201.4**). It is also illegal to carry them not concealed. Period. End of discussion. Kansas would prefer that your amateur go unarmed as of the time of this writing; however, it is probable that a law permitting the carrying of concealed weapons will be on the legislative agenda in 1996. Whether the measure will be passed remains to be seen.

Kentucky Attorney General's Office
Capitol Building, Room 116
Frankfort, KY 40601
(502) 564-7600

What Constitutes "Concealed"?

Is a shoulder holster concealed? Is a purse holster concealed?

A weapon carried in a shoulder holster is concealed unless no coat or shirt jacket of any kind is worn over it. A purse holster is always concealed.

If you are female, you are likely to feel conspicuous walking about with either a shoulder holster or a hip holster unconcealed by a jacket of any sort.

Citizen's Arrest

[standard wording]

Carrying a Weapon

Kentucky must comply with the rules of the federal Brady Law. According to a leaflet of commonly-asked questions about carrying guns in Kentucky, "A pistol or other deadly weapon may be lawfully carried in Kentucky so long as it is not concealed on or about one's person." However, this law does not apply to anybody who has been convicted of a felony, or to anybody who is using a weapon in a way "which threatens others, or causes alarm."

There are no provisions in Kentucky law for a permit to carry a concealed weapon, and "Kentucky does *not* recognize permits issued by other states for such purpose."

Kentucky Revised Statutes 527.020. Carrying concealed deadly weapon.

(4) A deadly weapon shall not be deemed concealed or about the person if it is located in a glove compartment, regularly installed in a motor vehicle by its manufacturer regardless of whether said compartment is locked, unlocked, or does not have a locking mechanism.

Simple and straightforward. If your amateur wants to carry a gun, he or she must carry it so that it is visible. This is easier for a man than a woman, and easier in warm weather than cold. (See sidebar above.)

Attorney General of **Louisiana**
P.O. Box 94005
New Orleans, LA 70804
(504) 342-7013

Citizen's Arrest
[standard wording]

Carrying a Weapon
Louisiana must comply with the rules of the federal Brady
Law. At present, its firearms laws are rather scant and vague,
and it is probable that firearms legislation, including concealed
weapon permits, will be on the 1996 agenda.

Attorney General of **Maine**
State House
Augusta, ME 04333
(207) 626-8800

Citizen's Arrest
Maine appears not to have any laws for or against citizen's
arrest, except for the detention (*not* arrest) of a shoplifter by a
merchant. Let your amateur use his or her own judgment, and
be prepared to back it up.

Carrying a Weapon
Maine has met or exceeded the standards of the federal
Brady Law and, therefore, is not required to comply with the
federal law. It prohibits ownership of firearms to a person convicted of any felony or violent misdemeanor, or who "has been
adjudicated in this State or under the laws of the United States
or any other state to have engaged in conduct as a juvenile
that, if committed by an adult, would have been a disqualifying
conviction."

This is an interesting example of a law made with the best of
intentions that will be extraordinarily hard to enforce, as juvenile
records in all states are normally sealed when the person reaches
the age of majority and can be kept open only by court order.

Maine also requires all firearms dealers to issue safety brochures to the purchasers, providing rules for the safe and responsible handling of firearms, and to post "the following warning in block letters not less than one inch in height:

ENDANGERING THE WELFARE OF A
CHILD IS A CRIME. IF YOU LEAVE A
FIREARM AND AMMUNITION WITHIN EASY
ACCESS OF A CHILD, YOU MAY BE SUB-
JECT TO FINE, IMPRISONMENT, OR BOTH.
"KEEP FIREARMS AND AMMUNITION
SEPARATE.
"KEEP FIREARMS AND AMMUNITION
LOCKED UP.
"USE TRIGGER LOCKS."

(Quotations from ME Rev. Stat. Ann. Title 15. 393, Chapter 17. 455A. and Chapter 252-A.2012.)

Nevertheless, Maine does permit civilians to carry concealed weapons.

More and more states are now passing laws such as the one this sign refers to. Too many children and teenagers are being killed while playing with firearms easily available at home when both parents are away. This situation will continue to increase as more and more mothers become breadwinners.

Attorney General of **Maryland**
200 St. Paul Place
Baltimore, MD 21202
(410) 576-6300

Citizen's Arrest

Maryland appears not to have any laws for or against citizen's arrest, except for shoplifting arrests by merchants. Let your amateur use his or her own judgment, and be prepared to back it up.

Carrying a Weapon

Maryland has met or exceeded the standards of the federal Brady Law and, therefore, is not required to comply with the federal law. The state maintains a Handgun Roster Board including representatives from law enforcement, the state judicial system, gun manufacturers or dealers, an NRA member, a representative of the Marylanders Against Handgun Abuse and three private citizens. The board is charged with deciding what handguns shall be permitted because they "are useful for legitimate sporting, self-protection, or law enforcement purposes" (36.j). Section 442 regulates to whom firearms shall be sold; as usual in most states, felons or violent misdemeanants, fugitives from justice, substance abusers, the mentally ill and those underage may not purchase firearms. Carrying of concealed firearms is not allowed.

Attorney General of **Massachusetts**
One Ashburton Place, 20th Floor
Boston, MA 02108
(617) 727-2200

Citizen's Arrest

Massachusetts appears not to have any laws for or against citizen's arrest, except for shoplifting arrests by a merchant. Let your amateur use his or her own judgment, and be prepared to back it up.

Carrying a Weapon

Massachusetts has met or exceeded the standards of the federal Brady Law and, therefore, is not required to comply with the federal law. Its laws are extremely lengthy and complicated; specifically, carrying a concealed weapon is illegal for civilians. We recommend that if your amateur is working there, check with an attorney or the owner of a gunshop, who can give you precise rules.

Attorney General of **Michigan**
P.O. Box 30212
525 West Ottawa Street
Lansing, MI 48909-0212
(517) 373-1110

Citizen's Arrest
Compiled Laws Annotated 764.16. Arrest by private person

Sec. 16. A private person may make an arrest—in the following situations:

[Part (a) is standard wording.]

(b) If the person to be arrested has committed a felony although not in the private person's presence.

(c) If the private person is summoned by a peace officer to assist the officer in making an arrest.

(d) If the private person is a merchant, an agent of a merchant, an employee of a merchant, or an independent contractor providing security for a merchant of a store and has reasonable cause to believe . . . regardless of whether the violation was committed in the presence of the private person.

The ellipses here represent the omission of five legal clauses which, summed up, refer to crimes committed against a merchant.

Carrying a Weapon

Michigan has met or exceeded the standards of the federal Brady Law and, therefore, is not required to comply with the federal law.

Michigan law provides that "a person shall not purchase, carry, or transport a pistol in this state without first having obtained a license for the pistol . . ." (**28.422. Sec. 2.**). In order to obtain such a permit, the person must meet requirements set forth in eleven different sections of the code, and: must be a citizen of the United States and a legal resident of Michigan; must not have a felony charge pending; must not have been adjudged insane or been committed to an inpatient or outpatient facility for treatment of mental illness; must have completed a pistol safety course; and must make a grade of at least seventy on a written test over the contents of the course.

All the above is just to *get* the gun. The same laws and more apply to carrying a weapon, along with fingerprinting, further records checks and no objections from "the supervisor of the township in which the applicant resides" (**28.426.2**). Under **28.426**. Sec. 6., the applicant must have "good reason to fear injury to his or her person or property, or has other proper reasons, and is a suitable person to be licensed."

Here's an interesting quirk: Michigan will grant an emergency thirty-day permit while the background check is being done if there is substantial reason to believe that the person is in danger. At present, no civilian may carry a concealed weapon; however, that question is expected to be on the 1996 legislative agenda.

Office of the Attorney General of **Minnesota**
102 State Capitol
St. Paul, MN 55155-1002
(612) 296-6196

Citizen's Arrest
Minnesota Code 629.30 ARRESTS; BY WHOM MADE; AIDING OFFICER.

Subdivision 1. **Definition**. Arrest means taking a person into custody that the person may be held to answer for a public offense. "Arrest" includes actually restraining a person or taking into custody a person who submits.

Subdivision 2. **Who may arrest**. An arrest may be made: . . .

(4) by a private person.

A private person shall aid a peace officer in executing a warrant when requested to do so by the officer.

Farther on, in section 629.36, the law spells out that a "bystander" may arrest "a person for breach of the peace," and the bystander then "may" deliver the person to the police officer. (Although the letter of the law here is "may," most likely anyone making a citizen's arrest and then failing to deliver the person to a police officer or judge ASAP could be charged with false arrest and/or kidnapping.)

Also, if "a public offense is committed in the presence of a judge, the judge may, by written or verbal order, command any person to arrest the offender, and then proceed as if the offender had been brought before the court on a warrant of arrest."

What can you think of to do with *that* law? I love it! I'm tempted to set a book in Minnesota just so I can use that law.

When there's no judge around, the law is a little more specific:

629.37 WHEN A PRIVATE PERSON MAY MAKE AN ARREST.

A private person may arrest another:

[Parts (1) and (2) are standard wording.]

(3) when a felony has in fact been committed, and the arresting person has reasonable cause for believing the person arrested to have committed it.

In section 609.06, the law specifically authorizes "reasonable force" . . . "when used by a person not a public officer in arresting another in the cases and in the manner provided by law and delivering the other to an officer competent to receive the other into custody. . . ."

And what is reasonable force? Ah, that's another story. "Reasonable force" is whatever a court decides is reasonable force. Your character, or any real-life or fictional law enforcement officer or private citizen trying to make an arrest, may have no more than two or three seconds to make a decision the courts may argue about for thirty years. But whatever decision the arresting person makes had better conform to whatever decision the courts wind up with. A few steps worse than catch-22? You bet. Police recruits are taught that it is easier to argue with a grand jury that wishes to indict you than with the coroner who has just pronounced you dead. In real life, it is best to avoid getting into this sort of situation to start with, unless it is totally unavoidable. In fiction, do whatever your plot calls for.

Carrying a Weapon

Minnesota must comply with the rules of the federal Brady Law.

624.714 subd. 2. "Applications for permits to carry shall be made to the chief of police or an organized full-time police department of the municipality where the applicant resides or to the county sheriff where there is no such local chief of police where the applicant resides."

The application requires complete identification of the person, permission for a records check to be made, completion of a firearms safety course, and "an occupation or personal safety hazard requiring a permit to carry." It is, however, statutorily legal to carry an unconcealed weapon around a "person's place of business, dwelling house, premises or on land possessed by the person. . . ." Civilians may not carry concealed weapons.

Office of the Attorney General of **Mississippi**
Carroll Gartin Justice Building
P.O. Box 220
Jackson, MS 39205-0220
(501) 359-3680

Citizen's Arrest
Mississippi Code Annotated. Sec. 99-3-7
ARREST WHEN MADE WITHOUT WARRANT:
    An officer or private citizen may arrest any person without warrant for an indictable offense committed, or a breach of the peace threatened or attempted in his presence; or
    [standard wording]
or on charge, made upon reasonable cause, of the commission of a felony by the person proposed to be arrested. And in all cases of arrests without warrant, the person making such arrest must inform the accused of the object and cause of arrest, except when he is in the actual commission of the offense or is arrested on pursuit.

Carrying a Weapon
    Mississippi must comply with the rules of the federal Brady Law; however, its five-day waiting period does not apply to persons with valid permits/licenses to carry handguns issued in the last five years.
    According to §97-37-1 of the Mississippi code, carrying a concealed weapon in Mississippi is forbidden unless the weapon is being concealed "in whole or in part within the confines of his own home or his place of business, or any real property associated with his home or business or within any motor vehicle."

Attorney General of **Missouri**
Supreme Court Building
101 High Street
P.O. Box 899
Jefferson City, MO 65102
(314) 751-3321

Citizen's Arrest
1994 Missouri Revised Statutes: Section 544.180. (Annotated)
Missouri does not have a statute law regarding citizen's arrest, making it either legal or illegal. However, in the case of Richardson vs. U.S. (1954), courts ruled that, "Under Missouri law a private person may make an arrest on showing of actual commission of a felony and reasonable grounds to suspect the accused."

Carrying a Weapon
1994 Missouri Revised Statutes: Chapter 571
Missouri has met or exceeded the standards of the federal Brady Law and, therefore, is not required to comply with the federal law.

Missouri law is unusually tough; a person must have a permit even to *acquire* a concealable weapon. The permit must be issued by the sheriff of the county in which the person lives, and the person must meet the following requirements: at least twenty-one years old, never convicted of a felony or a major misdemeanor, is not a fugitive from justice, has not been dishonorably discharged from the United States armed forces, has no history of substance abuse, has not been adjudged mentally incompetent and/or committed to a mental health facility, and can present proof of identification. After a background records check, which must be made within seven business days from the date of the application, the person has thirty days in which to purchase the weapon. After making the purchase, the applicant must return to the sheriff a description "including make, model and serial number" of the firearm.

Even though the law specifies that all of this rigamarole is required for the purchase of a concealable weapon, carrying a concealed weapon remains illegal. However, there seems to be a legal assumption in Missouri that a person would buy a concealable weapon only if he or she intends—legally or illegally—to carry it concealed.

Attorney General of **Montana**
Justice Building
215 North Sanders
Helena, MT 59620
(406) 444-2026

Citizen's Arrest
[standard wording with the addition of a shoplifting clause]

Carrying a Weapon
Montana must comply with the rules of the federal Brady Law. It prohibits possession of a silencer or a sawed-off firearm, and prohibits the use of a firearm by a child under fourteen unless the parent or a firearms safety instructor is present. Other than that, its laws are extraordinarily simple and nonspecific. Apparently your amateur can legally carry a weapon in Montana, but my guess is that he or she would be better off not doing it in the city.

Office of the Attorney General of **Nebraska**
2115 State Capitol Building
Lincoln, NE 68509-8920
(402) 471-2682

Citizen's Arrest
"Citizen's arrests are possible in the state of Nebraska if the citizen actually observes the perpetrator committing a misdemeanor, or if a felony has in fact been committed and the citizen has probable cause to believe that the individual to be arrested has committed that felony." (Personal letter from Laurie Smith Camp, Deputy Attorney General.)

Carrying a Weapon
Nebraska has met or exceeded the standards of the federal Brady Law and, therefore, is not required to comply with the federal law.

"Individuals are not allowed to carry concealed firearms, nor are convicted felons allowed to carry firearms." (Personal letter from Laurie Smith Camp, Deputy Attorney General.)

Office of the Attorney General of **Nevada**
Heroes Memorial Building, Capitol Complex
Carson City, NV 89701
(702) 687-4170

Citizen's Arrest
Nevada Code: Proceedings to Commitment
171.104 Arrest defined; by whom made. An arrest is the taking of a person into custody, in a case and in the manner authorized by law. An arrest may be made by a police officer or by a private person.
171.126 Arrest by private person. A private person may arrest another:
[Parts (1) and (2) are basically standard wording.]
(3) When a felony has been in fact committed, and he has reasonable cause for believing the person arrested to have committed it.
And here's an interesting one:
171.32 Person making arrest may summon assistance.
Any person making an arrest may orally summon as many persons as he deems necessary to aid him therein.

Nevada courts have ruled that it is not even necessary for the person making the arrest to make a formal declaration of arrest, as long as the person arrested understands that he is in the power of the one who is doing the arresting, and therefore submits to the arrest.

Carrying a Weapon
Nevada must comply with the rules of the federal Brady Law. Because of its extensive network of casinos and the fact

that organized crime tends to show up anywhere gambling (legal or illegal) is permitted, Nevada has had to make special laws prohibiting anyone not specially authorized to do so for public safety reasons from carrying firearms into a casino, although carrying a concealed weapon otherwise is legal by laws that vary from county to county. It also prohibits the sale of firearms to minors or convicted felons, and requires people authorized to carry firearms to carry their permit on them any time they are carrying the firearm. Many local jurisdictions have further requirements.

Attorney General of **New Hampshire**
208 State House Annex
Concord, NH 03301
(603) 271-3658

Citizen's Arrest
New Hampshire appears not to have any laws for or against citizen's arrest. Let your amateur use his or her own judgment, and be prepared to back it up.

Carrying a Weapon
New Hampshire has met or exceeded the standards of the federal Brady Law and, therefore, is not required to comply with the federal law.

It prohibits firearms sales to convicted felons, substance abusers and persons who sell illegal drugs whether or not they use drugs themselves. An interesting quirk here, which plugs a major loophole in the laws of many other states, is that no person may *sell* a firearm without having a license to do so, unless he or she sells the weapon *to* a licensed dealer or to a person he or she knows personally. Firearms may be carried only by "officers of the law, . . . persons holding hunters' licenses when lawfully engaged in hunting, . . . employees of express companies while on duty, or . . . watchmen while on duty" (159.17). Carrying a concealed weapon is legal when the proper authorization has been obtained.

Attorney General of **New Jersey**
Richard J. Hughes Justice Complex
Trenton, NJ 08625
(609) 984-9579

Citizen's Arrest

New Jersey appears not to have any laws for or against citizen's arrest, except for shoplifting detentions (*not* arrests) by a merchant. Let your amateur use his or her own judgment, and be prepared to back it up.

Carrying a Weapon

New Jersey has met or exceeded the standards of the federal Brady Law and, therefore, is not required to comply with the federal law. However, its laws are somewhat confusing, as in Chapter 2C:39-2: "When the legality of a person's conduct under this chapter depends on his possession of a license or permit or his having registered with or given notice to a particular person or agency, it shall be presumed that he does not possess such a license or permit or has not registered or given the required notice, until he establishes the contrary." That one, sooner or later, will land in the Supreme Court: it is a guilty-until-proven-innocent law, which is forbidden by the United States Constitution.

A person is required to get a firearms purchaser identification card before he or she may even purchase a firearm. Chapter 2C:58-4 establishes the rules under which a person may obtain a permit to carry a firearm: he or she must be of good character; must not be a convicted felon, substance abuser or suffering from mental illness; must not suffer from a physical defect or disease that would make handling of firearms unsafe; must not be under a court order forbidding him to purchase a firearm; and—this is interesting—a permit may not be issued "to any person where the issuance would not be in the interest of the public health, safety, or welfare" [2C:58-3.c.(5)]. Each permit permits a person to purchase only one handgun, but any reasonable number of rifles or shotguns. Although concealable weapons may be purchased, they may not be carried concealed by civilians.

Pawnbrokers here, as in some other states, are forbidden to lend money on firearms. This, of course, means that your character cannot find a murder weapon in a pawnshop. In fact, if you want to use anything in a pawnshop as a clue *anywhere*, you should ask for information about the governing laws from your local police department or, even better, a pawnbroker (if you can find one who will talk with you. Pawnbrokers tend to be very suspicious).

Attorney General of **New Mexico**
P.O. Drawer 1508
Santa Fe, NM 87504-1508
(505) 827-6000

Citizen's Arrest
New Mexico appears not to have any laws for or against citizen's arrest, except for shoplifting detentions (*not* arrests) by a merchant. Let your amateur use his or her own judgment, and be prepared to back it up.

Carrying a Weapon
New Mexico is required to comply with the rules of the federal Brady Law.

New Mexico spells out what is illegal in terms of firearms usage, but not what is legal. The following portions of the law apply to civilians:
30-7-2. Unlawful carrying of a deadly weapon.
A. Unlawful carrying of a deadly weapon consists of carrying a concealed loaded firearm or any other type of deadly weapon anywhere, except in the following cases:
(1) In the person's residence or on real property belonging to him as owner, lessee, tenant or licensee;
(2) in a private automobile or other private means of conveyance, for lawful protection of the person's or another's person or property.

Attorney General of **New York**
120 Broadway, 25th Floor
New York, NY 10271
(212) 416-8519

Citizen's Arrest
[standard wording]

Carrying a Weapon
New York has met or exceeded the standards of the federal Brady Law and, therefore, is not required to comply with the federal law.

New York's firearms laws are well known to be among the world's toughest, though, as in the District of Columbia, the number of illegal firearms on the streets of New York make the laws a sick joke. Probably more firearms are smuggled into the state of New York than into just about any other legal jurisdiction. The rules on who may not own a firearm alone fill up two $8\frac{1}{2}'' \times 11''$ sheets of paper, in very tiny three-column type. Licenses to carry firearms may be issued only under special circumstances, including a good reason for needing the permit, and even then they generally do not permit the weapon to be carried concealed. In New York City, a license to carry or even possess a pistol or revolver costs one hundred and seventy dollars for a two-year period; the permit to purchase a rifle or shotgun costs fifty-five dollars. Your amateur is poor? Then forget about guns—legal ones, anyway.

Attorney General of **North Carolina**
P.O. Box 629
Raleigh, NC 27602-0629
(919) 733-4723

Citizen's Arrest
According to a letter from Robin Pendergraft, Special Deputy Attorney General, "a private person may **detain** another person only under the circumstances outlined in N.C.G.S. §15A-404. A private person may **arrest** another individual while assisting a law-enforcement officer or requested to do so by a law-enforcement officer."

Carrying a Weapon
North Carolina is required to comply with the provisions of the federal Brady Law. Qualified citizens may obtain a permit

to carry a concealed handgun. Beyond that, the North Carolina Firearms Laws fill a booklet twenty-two pages long. If your character wants to carry a gun in North Carolina, I recommend you look the laws up yourself. They are complicated, but in general, as mentioned above, they follow the provisions of the federal Brady Law (see page 122).

Office of Attorney General of **North Dakota**
Capitol Tower, State Capitol
600 E. Boulevard Avenue
Bismarck, ND 58505-0040
(701) 328-2226

Citizen's Arrest
19-06-02. Who may make an arrest. An arrest may be made:

1. By a peace officer, under a warrant;

2. By a peace officer, without a warrant; or

3. By a private person.

North Dakota is one of the states that require any person, when requested, to aid an officer making an arrest. Given this law, it is not unreasonable to say that in some situations, citizen's arrest powers *must* be used.

29-06-20. When private person may arrest. A private person may arrest another:
[Parts 1 and 2 are basically standard wording.]
3. When a felony has been in fact committed, and he has reasonable ground to believe the person arrested to have committed it.

To sum up the rest of the law, the citizen "making the arrest must inform the person to be arrested of the intention to arrest him, and of the cause of the arrest, unless" the crime is in progress, the citizen is in pursuit, the person "flees or forcibly resists" before the citizen has a chance to tell him anything, or "the giving of such information will imperil the arrest."

And North Dakota law has an interesting little quirk:
29-06-22. When a private person may break into a

Deadly Force

Rules regarding the use of deadly force vary from state to state. In general, a person may use deadly force in the defense of himself and/or people he or she has a right to defend. Usually if the person has a way to retreat instead of using deadly force, an effort to retreat is required in place of force. In general, use of deadly force is *not* legal in defense of property.

building. A private person, in order to make an arrest where a felony was committed in his presence . . . if he is refused admittance after he has announced his purpose, may break open a door or window of any building in which the person to be arrested is, or is reasonably believed to be.

The citizen is then required to disarm the arrestee and to deliver him to a police officer or a magistrate.

Carrying a Weapon

North Dakota must comply with the requirements of the federal Brady Law; however, the federal five-day waiting period does not apply to persons with valid permits/licenses to carry handguns issued within the last five years.

Its laws relating to the carrying of handguns are interesting and rather unusual:

62.1-03-01. Carrying handgun—Restrictions—Exceptions
1. A handgun may be carried by a person not prohibited from possessing one by section 62.1-02-01 or any other state statute, in a manner not prohibited by section 62.1-02-10 if:

   a. Between the hours of one hour before sunrise and one hour after sunset, the weapon is carried unloaded and either in plain view or secured.

   b. Between the hours of one hour after sunset and one hour before sunset, the handgun is carried unloaded and secured.

Notice that this refers to unloaded and secured weapons. North Dakota issues concealed weapons licenses under the following circumstances:

62.1-04-03.a. The applicant has a valid reason for carrying the firearm or dangerous weapon concealed, including self-protection, protection of others or work-related needs.

To sum up the rest of the law, the applicant must have written approval from *both* the sheriff *and* the chief of police in the county and city where he or she lives. A background check is required, and the person must pass a test on weapons safety rules and the deadly force laws of North Dakota.

Attorney General of **Ohio**
State Office Tower
30 East Broad Street
Columbus, OH 43266-0410
(614) 466-3376

Citizen's Arrest
[standard wording]

Carrying a Weapon
Ohio must meet the requirements of the federal Brady Law. Ohio tactfully refers to being ineligible to carry a weapon as being "under disability." A person under disability is a fugitive from justice, is under indictment, has been convicted of a violent felony whether as an adult or a juvenile, is involved with distribution of illicit substances, is a substance abuser, or has been judged mentally incompetent. As of this writing, carrying a concealed weapon is still illegal; however, the 1996 legislative session expects to address the issue.

Attorney General of **Oklahoma**
2300 N. Lincoln Boulevard, Suite 112
Oklahoma City, OK 73105-4894
(405) 521-3921

Citizen's Arrest
[standard wording]

Carrying a Weapon

Oklahoma must meet the requirements of the federal Brady Law.

Convicted felons are prohibited from carrying firearms unless the felony was nonviolent and the person was granted a pardon and has graduated from a gunsmithing school. As of the time I looked up the law, that seemed to be the only prohibition other than age. Carrying a concealed weapon is statutorily legal.

Attorney General of **Oregon**
100 Justice Building
1162 Court Street N.E.
Salem, OR 97310
(503) 378-6002

Citizen's Arrest

133.220. Who may make arrest. An arrest may be effected by:

(1) A peace officer under a warrant;

(2) A peace officer without a warrant;

(3) A private person; or

(4) A federal officer.

133.225. Arrest by a private person. (1) A private person may arrest another person for any crime committed in the presence of the private person if the private person has probable cause to believe the arrested person committed the crime. A private person making such an arrest shall, without unnecessary delay, take the arrested person before a magistrate or deliver the arrested person to a peace officer.

(2) In order to make the arrest a private person may use physical force as is justifiable under ORS 161.225.

Carrying a Weapon

Oregon has met or exceeded the standards of the federal Brady Law and, therefore, is not required to comply with the federal law. A person who is otherwise qualified to have a firearm may carry it unconcealed in a belt holster, but he may not carry it concealed either on his person or within his vehicle without a permit. The concealed weapons law is too long and complicated to be quoted here. In general, it requires a person to be a citizen or a legal resident who has been in the county for six months and has indicated an intention to become a citizen. He or she must be at least twenty-one, must live in the county where the permit is to be issued, must have completed any acceptable firearms safety course, must never have been convicted of a crime, must not have any mental handicaps and must have no record of substance abuse. The license is issued by the sheriff after adequate identification, including fingerprints and photographs, is provided.

Attorney General of **Pennsylvania**
Strawberry Square, 16th Floor
Harrisburg, PA 171220
(717) 787-3391

Citizen's Arrest
Pennsylvania appears not to have any laws for or against citizen's arrest, except for shoplifting detentions (*not* arrests) by a merchant. Let your amateur use his or her own judgment and be prepared to back it up.

Carrying a Weapon
Pennsylvania has met or exceeded the standards of the federal Brady Law and, therefore, is not required to comply with the federal law.

It forbids firearm ownership to a convicted violent felon, person under eighteen, substance abuser or person of unsound mind. Carrying of concealed weapons is permitted, but check with the specific jurisdiction as to its laws. Pawnbrokers are forbidden to make loans on firearms.

Department of the Attorney General
State of **Rhode Island and Providence Plantations**
72 Pine Street
Providence, RI 02908
(401) 274-4400

Citizen's Arrest

The state of Rhode Island sent us a photocopy of a page from *Black's Law Dictionary* defining citizen's arrest, indicating that Rhode Island follows the rules set forth therein. This additional comment comes from the Rhode Island General Laws: **12-7-16. Arrest of seizure after commission of offense.**—The authority given to any one to arrest any person or seize anything, while the person is actually engaged or the thing is actually used or employed in the commission of any offense, shall not be so construed as to prevent, if not so arrested or seized, the arrest of the person or the seizure of the thing after the commission of the offense, upon due process of law.

This is one of the more confusing state laws. As best I can determine without being an attorney, it means that although anybody has the right to arrest a person committing an unlawful act and to seize the weapons or instruments being used in that act, the criminal does not necessarily have to be caught in the act and the weapons or instruments do not necessarily have to be seized only when they are in use. The person may be arrested, and the weapons or instruments seized, at any time in the future, in a lawful manner.

Carrying a Weapon

Rhode Island has met or exceeded the standards of the federal Brady Law and, therefore, is not required to comply with the federal law.

Rhode Island's handgun laws are too lengthy and complicated to be quoted here. A person wanting a license to carry a concealable weapon must fill in a four-page form and provide a typed letter of explanation as to why the permit is needed, two photographs, the signature of the chief of police in the city in which the person resides, proof of completion of a firearms safety course, and a full set of fingerprints along with twenty dollars. Here your brilliant amateur is at the mercy of the police chief: the police chief may decide that the person doesn't need to carry a weapon and, in that case, the person can't get a permit.

In January 1995, Rhode Island published a comparison between the Brady Law and Rhode Island Law with the proviso that in each case, the tougher law applies. Rhode Island law

Lawful Arrest

What is required for an arrest to be lawful when it takes place at a different time and place from that of the crime? If you are thinking of a specific situation, as of course you are when writing fiction, you would do well to discuss the matter with an attorney from that jurisdiction. However, an arrest at a different time and place from that of the offense generally must be made only with a warrant or with the knowledge that a warrant has been issued. Normally such an arrest can be made only by a law enforcement officer. However, if a person has knowledge that a crime has been committed and that this is the person who committed it, in most *but not all* jurisdictions, a citizen's arrest is legal.

covers handguns, rifles and shotguns; has a mandatory seven-day waiting period, requires the purchaser of a firearm to be twenty-one or over; requires a pistol revolver safety course; makes the police chief in the city or town where the gun is sold responsible for making a criminal records check; and requires the following identification questions to be answered: name, address, date of birth, height, weight, color of eyes, color of hair, scars, tattoos and other marks.

Rhode Island provides these disqualifications: record of violence in any state, record of controlled substance abuse in any state; or record of mental illness or alcoholism. An alien may not purchase a firearm unless he has been in the United States for ten years or more.

Attorney General of **South Carolina**
1000 Assembly Street
Columbia, SC 29211
(803) 734-3970

Citizen's Arrest
[standard wording]

What Is a Plea of Nolo?

It is a slang term for the legal term "nolo contendere," which may be given instead of a plea of either guilty or not guilty. It carries the meaning of "we won't argue about whether I'm guilty or not guilty; just sentence me and let me pay the fine and get out of here." People involved in law enforcement generally assume that nobody would plead "nolo" who wasn't in fact guilty. This assumption is not necessarily correct.

Carrying a Weapon

South Carolina must meet the requirements of the federal Brady Law.

It permits a person convicted of a crime or violence to possess a rifle or shotgun but not a pistol. Pistols may be purchased only by persons who have filled out an application in triplicate, containing full identification. South Carolina does not permit the carrying of concealed weapons by civilians.

Attorney General of **South Dakota**
500 East Capitol
Pierre, SD 57501-5070
(605) 773-3215

Citizen's Arrest

[standard wording]

Carrying a Weapon

South Dakota must meet the provisions of the federal Brady Law; however, the federal five-day waiting period does not apply to persons with valid permits/licenses to carry handguns issued within the last five years. A person who does not already have a valid permit to carry a concealed pistol cannot buy the weapon until he has applied for the permit, which cannot be issued if he has ever pled guilty or nolo to a crime of violence.

Attorney General of **Tennessee**
450 James Robertson Parkway
Nashville, TN 37243-0485
(615) 741-3491

Citizen's Arrest
[standard wording]

Carrying a Weapon
Tennessee has met or exceeded the standards of the federal
Brady Law and, therefore, is not required to comply with the
federal law.
Tennessee State Code 39.17.1315.(b) (1) (A) . . . . [A] person
wishing to carry a handgun shall apply to the sheriff of the
county of such person's principal place of residence for a handgun permit. The sheriff shall issue such a permit and a written
directive to persons not prohibited from purchasing firearms
authorizing the person to carry a handgun; provided, that the
person meets all the requirements of this section. The sheriff
may, for good cause and in the reasonable exercise of discretion,
deny a permit.

The law goes on to mention specific exceptions: past or
present addiction to alcohol or drugs; past or present hospitalization or other treatment for alcohol or drug addiction; past or present
hospitalization for mental illness; a physical infirmity preventing
safe operation of a handgun—EXCEPT that the sheriff can issue
a permit anyway, at the sheriff's own discretion. (What a lot you
can do with this! Does your amateur get along with the sheriff?
Voila! Instant handgun permit! Is your amateur a perennial thorn
in the sheriff's side? Then he or she probably won't get a firearms
permit in the next two hundred years.)

The law does require firearms training of some sort in a
state-approved firearms course, and the person must carry at least
$50,000 in liability insurance related to firearms usage.

Attorney General of **Texas**
Capitol Station, P.O. Box 12548
Austin, TX 78711-2548
(512) 463-2191

Citizen's Arrest
Vernon's Texas Statutes Annotated. Art. 14.01.
OFFENSE WITHIN VIEW.

A peace officer or any other person may, without warrant, arrest an offender when the offense is committed in his presence or within his view, if the offense is one classified as a felony, or as an offense against the public peace.

Carrying a Weapon

Texas is required to meet the requirements of the federal Brady Law. Texas changed its firearms laws so close to the publication date of this book that it was not possible for us to obtain a written copy of the law. However, the law now provides for issuance of a concealed weapon permit, following the normal Brady rules and requiring training both in the safe handling of weapons and in nonviolent settling of disputes. And Texas has added a new quirk to the law: any business may make its own rules as to whether or not a firearm may be carried concealed into that place of business. A cafeteria chain—in one of whose cafeterias there was a horrifying multiple murder during the busiest part of the day several years ago—promptly posted a sign stating that it will permit firearms to be carried. There had been numerous complaints after the murder by patrons who normally carried firearms but had left them in their cars in deference to the state law as it was then, which forbade firearms to be carried into an eating establishment.

You as a writer can probably find uses for rules either for or against the carrying of a firearm into whatever place of business you have in mind.

Attorney General of **Utah**
236 State Capitol
Salt Lake City, UT 84111
(801) 538-9600

Citizen's Arrest
Utah Code of Criminal Procedure
77-7-3. By private persons.
[standard wording]

Carrying a Weapon

Utah has met or exceeded the standards of the federal Brady Law and, therefore, is not required to comply with the federal law.

Utah Code Annotated. Section 53-5-704.

(1) The division or its designated agent shall issue a permit to carry a concealed firearm for lawful self defense to an applicant who is 21 years of age or older within 60 days after receiving an application and upon proof that the person applying is of good character. The permit is valid throughout the state, without restriction, for two years.

The law further requires that for a person to be issued a permit, he or she must have been trained in the use of the firearm and must present two recent dated photographs, two sets of fingerprints, a five-year employment history and a five-year residential history. (If your character is a rambler or self-employed, this can present problems.)

Office of the Attorney General of **Vermont**
Pavilion Office Building
109 State Street
Montpelier, VT 05602
(802) 828-3171

Citizen's Arrest

Vermont appears not to have any laws for or against citizen's arrest. Let your amateur use his or her own judgment, and be prepared to back it up.

Carrying a Weapon

Vermont has met or exceeded the standards of the federal Brady Law and, therefore, is not required to comply with the federal law. But its only rule related to the carrying of concealed weapons is that they may not be carried with the intent of injuring another person.

Attorney General of **Virginia**
Commonwealth of Virginia
900 East Main Street
Richmond, VA 23216
(804) 786-2071

Citizen's Arrest
Virginia appears not to have any laws for or against citizen's arrest, except for shoplifting arrests by a merchant. Let your amateur use his or her own judgment, and be prepared to back it up.

Carrying a Weapon
Virginia has met or exceeded the standards of the federal Brady Law and, therefore, is not required to comply with the federal law.
A person who is not a police officer may be allowed to carry a firearm under certain circumstances:
Crimes Involving Health and Safety
18.2-308.D Any person twenty-one years of age or older may apply in writing to the clerk of the circuit court of the county or city in which he resides for a two-year permit to carry a concealed handgun. The application shall be made under oath before a notary or other person qualified to take oaths and shall be made on a form prescribed by the Supreme Court, requiring only that information necessary to determine eligibility for the permit. The court, after consulting the law-enforcement authorities of the county or city and receiving a report from the Central Criminal Records Exchange, shall issue the permit within forty-five days of receipt of the completed application unless it appears that the applicant is disqualified, except that any permit issued prior to July 1, 1996, shall be issued within ninety days of receipt of the completed application.
The law goes on to spell out categories of persons ineligible to obtain a gun permit: any person who is ineligible to receive a gun permit under the laws of any other state; any person who has been deemed mentally incompetent, unless his "competency was restored" more than five years before the date of application; any person who has committed two or more

misdemeanors, not counting traffic infractions; any person addicted to any drugs; an alcoholic or a person who has been convicted of public drunkenness within the three-year period immediately preceding the application; an illegal alien; a fugitive from justice; a person who has received a dishonorable discharge from the armed forces of the United States; any person whose behavior is such that the sheriff, chief of police or attorney for the Commonwealth believes that person should not be allowed to carry a gun; any person who has been convicted of any crime involving firearms within the three-year period preceding application; any person who has a felony charge pending; any person who has been convicted of stalking; any person who has received inpatient mental health or substance abuse treatment; and any person who makes a false statement in his application for a permit. Furthermore, the court may "require proof that the applicant has demonstrated competence with a handgun" and has attended any one of several approved firearms safety courses.

Several of the clauses in this law can be particularly useful for a writer to play with.

Attorney General of **Washington**
P.O. Box 40100
Olympia, WA 98504
(206) 753-6200

Citizen's Arrest

Washington appears not to have any laws for or against citizen's arrest. Let your amateur use his or her own judgment, and be prepared to back it up.

Carrying a Weapon

Washington must meet the requirements of the federal Brady Law.

Its laws prohibit gun ownership by certain classes of undesirables; in general, carrying a concealed weapon is legal, but check with local jurisdictions you intend to write about.

Attorney General of **West Virginia**
State Capitol
Charleston, WV 25305
(304) 558-2021

Citizen's Arrest
　　West Virginia appears not to have any laws for or against citizen's arrest, except for shoplifting detentions (*not* arrests) by a merchant. Let your amateur use his or her own judgment, and be prepared to back it up.

Carrying a Weapon
　　West Virginia must meet the requirements of the federal Brady Law.
　　It prohibits the possession of deadly weapons by a convicted felon, a person dishonorably discharged from any of the armed forces of the United States, a person who is mentally incompetent, an illegal alien or a substance abuser. Carrying a concealed weapon is permitted, but check with the local jurisdiction you intend to write about for location-specific laws.

Attorney General of **Wisconsin**
Department of Justice
123 West Washington Avenue
P.O. Box 7857
Madison, WI 53707-7857
(608) 267-2223

Citizen's Arrest
　　Wisconsin appears not to have any laws for or against citizen's arrest, except for shoplifting detentions (*not* arrests) by a merchant. Let your amateur use his or her own judgment, and be prepared to back it up.

Carrying a Weapon
　　Wisconsin has met or exceeded the standards of the federal Brady Law and, therefore, is not required to comply with the federal law.

It requires a records search before a firearm is sold; the firearms dealer must pay eight dollars to the state for each records search. No firearms may be purchased by a convicted felon or a person suffering from mental disease or defect. Wisconsin does not permit the carrying of concealed weapons by citizens.

Attorney General of **Wyoming**
123 Capitol Building
Cheyenne, WY 82002
(307) 777-7841

Citizen's Arrest
Wyoming Statutes. Title 7, Sec. 156.
CITIZENS MAY MAKE ARREST.
Any person not an officer may, without warrant, arrest any person if a petit larceny or felony has been committed, and there is reasonable ground to believe the person arrested guilty of such offense, and may detain him until a legal warrant can be obtained.

Carrying a Weapon
Wyoming must meet the requirements of the federal Brady Law. It requires firearms dealers to register every firearm that comes into their possession and to cause the purchaser of that firearm to sign the register. The city of Cheyenne, but not the state, prohibits the possession of a firearm by convicted felons, fugitives from justice, illegal aliens, mental incompetents and substance abusers. Wyoming permits the carrying of concealed weapons, but a good many cities have their own laws, so check carefully before you write.

Possessions and Territories of the United States
We did not search the statutes of the possessions and territories of the United States. However, we have provided addresses if you need to check on legalities in these areas.

Attorney General of **American Samoa**
P.O. Box 7
Pago Pago, American Samoa (AS) 96799

Attorney General of **Guam**
Judicial Center Building
120 West O'Brien Drive
Agana, Guam (GU) 96910
(671) 475-3324

Attorney General of the **Northern Mariana Islands**
Mariana Island
Saipan, MP 96950
(670) 332-4311

Attorney General of **Puerto Rico**
Department of Justice
P.O. Box 192
San Juan, Puerto Rico (PR) 00902

Attorney General of the **Virgin Islands**
No. 48B-50C Kronprindsens Gade
St. Thomas, Virgin Islands (VI) 00802

What the Law Allows: Canada

Citizen's Arrest
Canadian laws on citizen's arrest, since they also are based on English common law, are somewhat similar to those of the United States, but they are not exactly like those of any state. Canadian Criminal Code Sec. 494:
(1) Any one may arrest without warrant
(a) a person whom he finds committing an indictable offense; or

Canadian Criminal Code

Since the Criminal Code is federal it applies to all provinces in Canada.

Troy Demers
Department of Justice
Ottawa, Canada

(b) a person who, on reasonable grounds, he believes
   (i) has committed a criminal offence, and
   (ii) is escaping from and freshly pursued by persons who have lawful authority to arrest that person.
(2) Any one who is
   (a) the owner or a person in lawful pursuit of property, or
   (b) a person authorized by the owner or by a person in lawful possession of property, may arrest without warrant a person whom he finds committing a criminal offence on or in relation to that property.
(3) Any one other than a peace officer who arrests a person without warrant shall forthwith deliver the person to a peace officer.

Carrying a Weapon

Canadian Criminal Code sec. 110 states it as follows:
(2) A permit may be issued only where the person authorized to issue it is satisfied that the applicant therefor [sic] requires the restricted weapon to which the application relates
   (a) to protect life;
   (b) for use in connection with his lawful profession or occupation;
   (c) for use in target practice under the auspices of a shooting club approved for the purposes of this section by the Attorney General of the province in which the premises of the shooting club are located; or
   (d) for use in target practice in accordance with the conditions attached to the permit.

Canadian law further requires that *all* firearms be registered, and a mandatory four-year prison sentence and lifetime prohibition against the possession of a firearm be applied to anyone committing any of the following crimes:

- attempted murder
- manslaughter
- criminal negligence causing death
- robbery
- kidnapping
- hostage-taking
- sexual assault with a weapon
- aggravated sexual assault
- extortion
- discharge of a firearm with intent to cause harm

Furthermore, firearms must be stored unloaded and either rendered inoperable by a secure locking device or in a locked case or a locked room. And, if a police officer has reason to believe that a person's ownership of a firearm is placing that person or someone else in danger, the officer may seize the firearm without a warrant if the situation is such that taking the time to get a warrant might not be practicable.

Because Canada contains a large rural population, many of whom rely on hunting for food, partial exemption from the law will be provided in such situations.

E I G H T
THE RIGHT TO PRIVACY AND OTHER MYTHS

Every government collects tons of information every year; theoretically, a large percentage of that information should be returned to the people. More tons of information are collected by various privately owned but government-regulated agencies. As a writer, you have a particularly important position in this two-way flow of information: you create information (because even the most ephemeral of novels tells much about the civilization that created it) and you use information. None of us could function without our trusty library. How can you lay your hands upon some of the multitude of information the government has collected? How can your amateur detective use it?

This varies according to a number of things. Are you looking for information from the United States government? Some agencies are easier to work with than others. Are you looking for information from individual state governments? The laws vary from state to state. If you're asking for information from

Canada, at least the federal law and provincial law are likely to be the same most of the time (though I wouldn't be too sure about Quebec). If you're dealing with any other foreign country, you may have a lot more trouble: most of the letters we have sent over the years asking for information from foreign governments, or from their embassies, seem to have dropped into a dark hole (though Libya did send me a very nice picture of the wrong statue). If you're dealing with a private company, you might be just about home free, or you might be told that information will never, under any circumstances, be made available.

Obtaining Information From U.S. Government Agencies

The first place to look, before you even start thinking about things like the Freedom of Information Act (FOIA), is the closest government repository library. Most states have at least one of these libraries, usually but not always in their largest state-funded university. Your local library can tell you where your closest repository library is. Be forewarned: The filing system of such a library is completely different from either the Dewey decimal or Library of Congress classification system, and you'll probably need a guide the first few times you go there.

One of the things you can get there is a postcard to fill out and mail in, putting you on various mailing lists from the Government Printing Office. There is a staggering amount of information available in government publications, and most of it is reasonably priced and updated regularly. That is the information the government wants you to have and works hard to make it easy for you to get. When you start trying to access information the government actively does *not* want you to have, things can get downright hairy. With no intention of discouraging you—after all, not all FOIA requests run into problems— we'll take time to discuss some of the roadblocks.

These roadblocks are not always the government's fault, or yours, or anybody else's. Part of the trouble is that two different laws often come nose to nose: The Right to Privacy Act puts certain limits on what information can be released, some of which is supposed to be available under the Freedom of

Information Act. This leaves bureaucrats, especially the nondecision-making echelons, totally baffled as to what they may and may not do. So the widespread belief that citizens would have easier access to government records when the Freedom of Information Act was passed has not always proven to be correct. There are a couple of problems with this belief.

First, some agencies—particularly, but not always, law enforcement agencies—are unwilling to release information, no matter what the law says. They may put immense roadblocks in people's paths, sometimes requiring the citizen to provide the title, file number and location of the document sought, which the citizen could not possibly know without having the document. They may require ridiculous fees for copying, at times up to five dollars a page. They may require the interested citizen to go and search the archives personally, which may be physically and financially impossible. Repeatedly, people interested in chasing down information have had to resort to lawsuits; this has been the case in some areas in which that particular government agency insists it has no interest. The book *Clear Intent*, discussed in the sidebar on page 171 and a subsequent paragraph, has provided several good examples of this kind of situation. It is necessary reading for anybody, no matter how uninterested in UFOs he or she might be, who hopes to get information released from an agency that prefers not to release information.

Sometimes the reasons for refusal are not stated or make no sense whatever; in other cases, there is no discernible reason for refusing to release the information. When Hillary Johnson set out to write *Osler's Web*, which intended to do for Chronic Fatigue Syndrome what Randy Shilts' *And the Band Played On* did for AIDS, she made a routine request, under the Freedom of Information Act, for documents from the National Institute of Health. Attorneys working *pro bono*—that is, without charge and in the public interest—worked with her to be sure that her request was properly presented. She and her lawyers even met face to face with agency representatives. *Two years later* the documents still had not shown up. By that time, Johnson had been dropped by her original publisher, had run out of money and had given up her apartment, moving in with her mother.

UFOs and the Government

Of approximately three thousand pages of information related to Unidentified Flying Objects that were released in the first four years of the Freedom of Information Act, approximately one thousand were released only after complicated lawsuits. Some remain unavailable even after lawsuits. As highly reputable scientist J. Allen Hynek commented in 1983, "Not all existing . . . documents in the possession of these intelligence agencies have . . . been released. . . . Of special interest would be those documents held by the National Security Agency whose release the courts denied, and which denial was the subject of the case the Supreme Court refused to hear. This upheld . . . the claim of the lower courts that the release of said documents would jeopardize national security. . . . as one national newspaper proclaimed in a front-page headline, 'If There Are No UFOs, Why All the Secrecy?' "

The documents never showed up. No sensible reason for the refusal to release them was ever given, and *Osler's Web* finally went to press without vital information about a life-destroying communicative disease from the National Institute of Health. Some of the refused information may be unimportant to most of the world but critically important to the person asking for it.

Second, many agencies—whether or not for good reason—take ridiculously long periods of time to respond to citizen requests. When the requested document finally arrives, it may be so censored as to be totally useless. For example, in numerous UFO books including Lawrence Fawcett and Barry Greenwood's *Clear Intent*, authors have noted that often when the documents finally do arrive, so much has been deleted (officially for security reasons or to protect the privacy of other people) that what remains amounts to little more than a collection of *is, was, the* and so forth.

Sometimes the information may truly not be available. A major fire about thirty years ago in a U.S. government storage facility in St. Louis, Missouri, destroyed over half of all the

Army personnel records for a time period that included World War II. If you need some of these records, all the Army good will in the world can't do *you* any good. The records don't exist. A destructive fire is a reason anybody can accept for why records don't exist. But sometimes the reason why is less acceptable.

Along these lines, a scandal recently erupted in the Internal Revenue Service. Seven years ago, historian Shelley Davis was hired "to catalog the historical records of an agency that is ubiquitous in American life and chronicle its past" (Combined News Services, December 16, 1995). Davis, formerly an Air Force historian, was appalled to find that there were almost no records after *1930*: "The agency that forces millions of taxpayers to keep meticulous financial records . . . dumps its own historical files in a basement or in desk drawers—or shreds them." Although the agency is required by law to "turn over records of historical significance to the National Archives, [it] had last done so in 1971—and those papers involved tax-assessment lists from 1909 through 1917."

An official spokesman for the IRS claims that two different federal laws attempt to govern it; one requires the records to be turned over to the National Archives, but the other prohibits individual tax information from being released to any other person or agency.

Davis resigned. She will not be replaced. The IRS has decided it does not *want* an historian.

Don't count on obtaining any information under the FOIA from the IRS, other than copies of your own past tax forms, which you don't have to refer to the FOIA in requesting. They'll gladly send those to you.

What to Ask for in a Freedom of Information Act Request

Be as specific as possible, as the government receives thousands of such requests and sometimes must search through millions of records—and government records are perhaps even more likely to be misfiled than records of private companies. Include names, dates, places and any file numbers you know in your request.

It is safest to ask to be notified, before the search is made, of the fees to be charged for search, duplication and review, so you won't find yourself hit with an immense bill from the government. Ask that if your request is denied, the agency cite the specific reasons why it can't or won't release the information and how you can appeal. If you ever choose to request *your* file from the FBI, assuming that you have one (most people don't unless they have been involved in either questionable activities or law enforcement) the bureau wants you to include the following information: your complete name, current address, date and place of birth, a notarized signature and a daytime telephone number. It also requests any additional information available such as previous addresses, places of employment, aliases and so on, which you believe may assist the FBI in locating the information.

You may safely assume that any other federal agency will want at least this much information and possibly more, and this is a request only for information about *yourself.* Information about anyone else, unless you can provide an extremely good reason (preferably a court order) for it to be released to you, is totally unavailable under the provisions of the Right to Privacy Act. However the FBI will, under rare circumstances, release information about a person who is dead if the person making the request has an acceptable reason for requesting it.

What Can You Get?

Theoretically, under the federal FOIA, you may get any public record provided it does not compromise national security, does not list agency rules and practices, is not a statutory exemption, is not confidential business information or internal memoranda, does not involve personal or medical files, does not involve law enforcement investigations, is not a banking report, and does not contain information about oil and gas wells. You can also get copies of federal trial transcripts, but those were available even before the FOIA. The most common reason for denial of an information request is that release of that information is likely to violate national security or someone else's right to privacy.

How Long Does It Take?

Theoretically, it takes ten days. In reality . . . the ten days are counted until the *first* response to the request, which often may be no more than a request from the agency for you to supply more information.

One of the authors of this book, knowing that the FBI has a file on her, decided to test-drive the FOIA. She played more than fair. When she submitted her request, she told the FBI that it was being made so that the speed and accuracy of the response could be put in a book called *Amateur Detectives* to be published by Writer's Digest Books. This would let the readers have some idea of what kind of response they could expect. She also asked for any information the FBI would specifically like to provide our readers.

She pointed out that she knew a good bit of what was in the file on her, provided several names of FBI agents who had placed information in the file, and even told the FBI which agent had placed which piece of information. Her original letter was mailed on July 10, 1995. In August, a letter dated July 24, which would have almost met the reply-within-ten-days rule if it had been mailed right after it was written, arrived from the FBI. It contained a form listing information needed for her request to be processed, along with her original letter and mailing envelope, and her specific questions highlighted.

The author duly, and immediately, provided all the information requested. In late August she received a second form letter, informing her that the search was being made and the information would be supplied as soon as possible.

In March 1996, more than nine months after filing her request, she received a letter (dated in February) telling her that due to the volume of requests the FBI has received, it would take more than two years from the date of the letter for the FBI to provide any information at all to her from her file or to anyone else from his or her file. She has received no information about the FOIA and no information about anything the FBI would like to tell her readers. (Fortunately that was not the only source of information about the FOIA.)

It is only fair to note that there have been two government shutdowns in the intervening months resulting from budgetary problems, so this particular test may not have been as fair as one could wish. But the experiences we have described that other people have had indicates that in many situations, though certainly not all, it can be very difficult to get information.

FOIA Delays and the Amateur Detective

Can you use this very difficulty in fiction? I can think of half a dozen ways of using it. What if your amateur needs information he or she can't get? What if your amateur has been the victim of false information when his or her file got tangled with the file of somebody else with the same name? What if your amateur, while trying to cope with everything else the plot is throwing at him or her, also has to cope with an overly helpful or unhelpful government bureaucrat? You can use this type of situation for drama or humor, to build the character or to advance the plot.

But if your amateur detective absolutely must have access to government files, there are always ways to get at them. Just watch the headlines. Over the last five years, I have seen news reports of people as young as junior high hacking into everything from school grade records to university E-mail systems to national defense databases. If your amateur is a good enough computer hacker to break into computerized files—and you are reasonably sure the files they wanted *are* computerized and available on-line—your amateur can get at them that way, no matter what the level of security is assumed to be. Remember, you don't have to know how to do it yourself to let your amateur do it. And there are multitudes of state, county and city files that might be more useful to your amateur than federal files. There are also assorted state Freedom of Information Acts and Right to Privacy Acts that supplement and complement the federal act.

The Individual States

Following is *only a sample* of individual state laws regarding rights of privacy and freedom of information laws. We are concentrating on Florida because its laws seem reasonably representative of those being passed by all of the various states. In addition, we've picked up a few interesting quirks from other states. Bear in mind that this is an area that is in flux. Before the federal FOIA was passed, in many cases in some states what was and was not "a matter of public record" was partly determined by custom rather than by law. Since passage of the federal FOIA, states in general are tending to pass laws very similar to those passed by the federal government. To learn the exact status of such laws in your state, call your state attorney general (see phone numbers in chapter seven) and ask where you can obtain copies of the laws.

The fact that the laws exist does not necessarily mean they are followed. Despite the existence of "Sunshine Laws"—that is, laws requiring the meetings of certain governmental agencies on all levels of government to be open to visitors—not a day goes by without news reports that some agency, somewhere, is illegally closing its meetings to individuals and/or the press. If your amateur needs to know what happened behind those closed doors, he or she had better be good at finding the right people and asking the right questions.

In 1992, the Brechner Center for Freedom of Information, the Center for Governmental Responsibility at the University of Florida, the First Amendment Foundation and the St. Petersburg *Times* joined forces to produce an informative booklet explaining Florida's new laws governing freedom of information and the right to privacy. The noncopyrighted booklet was made available for general distribution by the state of Florida. You can probably get a copy from an interlibrary loan; it will be quite useful even if your story is not set in Florida as the Florida law is a good sample of laws in all states. It sets forth a complete explanation of what is and is not considered a matter of public record and hence available to the public, and what continues to be unavailable. It gives reasonable explanations if something is unavailable.

Generally, the public has access to: most original police reports (though not necessarily the follow-up reports, especially if they record ongoing investigations or internal affairs problems); most but not all personnel records of government employees including their payroll status; most records of abuse or abandonment of children or adults unless they are still part of an ongoing investigation; most written information exchanged between a government agency and its attorneys unless the information is relevant to an ongoing lawsuit; most tape recordings of incoming calls to police departments; most information about governmental units' budgets and their plans for new buildings; and most of the records of the Florida Commission on Ethics.

However, this list cannot be taken as a blanket authority to release everything. There are things specifically exempted from release, some of which (such as birth records) we found rather unexpected. In common with most states, the release of names of sexual abuse victims and police informants is prohibited. Juvenile and adoption records can be released only in very special situations, usually involving court orders. Student records may be released only to students, the parents of a minor student, and otherwise with the signed permission of the student. Information "necessary to the security and integrity" of the Florida Lottery logically cannot be released, but we were surprised to learn of the prohibition of release of reports of "public health significance." Certainly the *names* of the subjects of the reports should not be released, but writers and the public have legitimate need to know in relation to the incidence and demographics of such diseases.

It is reasonable to prohibit, as Florida does, any information about ongoing negotiations for the purchase of real estate by any government agencies, tax information, and home addresses and telephone numbers of law enforcement officers and certain other government officials. But it's a little harder to understand the reasoning behind Florida's prohibition of the release of booking information of publicly owned convention centers, arenas and so forth.

Some state agency records are deemed confidential by federal law even if they are open under Florida's Public Records Law. An example is drug treatment records of public agencies receiving federal funds.

In general, on the state and federal level throughout the United States, court proceedings, other than juvenile courts, are always open to the public. This requirement dates from the earliest days of the American republic and was originally intended to prevent Star Chamber situations—which still occur in some nations—when a person may be arrested in the middle of the night and never heard from again.

However, the Florida Supreme Court has ruled, in connection with the right to privacy, that courts may be closed on rare occasions. This ruling has been echoed in many states. In a criminal case, such closure may occur only if the situation is such that open court would "prevent a serious and imminent threat to the administration of justice." Usually, that means that the person on trial is so loved or hated that mob rule may interfere with the judicial process. Even then it is permitted only if no less restrictive measures would work and closure would protect the defendant's rights better than any other possible way of dealing with the situation.

Civil court is less difficult to close; such closure is done only if it is necessary: to protect trade secrets; to avoid embarrassing semi-involved people who are not parties to the suit (such as children in a divorce court); to prevent nullification of rights to privacy laws; or to "protect a compelling government interest, such as national security or the identities of confidential informants." ("Protect national security in *civil* court"? That one puzzled us, too, until we remembered how many industrial espionage cases are handled in civil court rather than criminal court.) Before ordering closure in a civil proceeding, the judge must also find that no reasonable alternative is available and then use the least restrictive closure necessary to accomplish the stated purpose.

So far as we know, however, grand jury proceedings are closed in every state. Also, whether or not a jury is sequestered, the members of the jury are routinely ordered not to discuss the case among themselves or with anyone else until after the verdict is rendered.

Georgia provides an additional specification related to criminal courts. A court exhibit (that is, weapons, drawings, charts, photographs and so forth used in a trial) may "not be opened to public inspection without approval of the judge assigned to the case." However, if the public is not allowed to see the actual exhibit, the "custodian of such exhibit shall, upon request, provide one or more of the following representations of the exhibit:

(1) A photograph;

(2) A photocopy;

(3) A facsimile; or

(4) Another reproduction (**50-18-71.1**)"

These provisions seem to defeat the purpose of not opening the exhibit for inspection to start with, while putting more work on the already overburdened clerk of the court.

Georgia provides that public disclosure is not required for medical or veterinary records; prosecution and investigative material, the disclosure of which would "endanger the life or physical safety of any person or persons, or disclose the existence of a confidential surveillance or investigation"; or police records "other than initial police arrest records, accident reports, and incident reports" (**50-18-72.a.3** and **a.4**). After the investigation and/or all litigation involving the case has been concluded, the information may then be released. This provision can be used to get your amateur detective into a world of trouble: If he or she has been acting as an unofficial undercover informant and his or her cover is suddenly blown, danger may stream from all sides.

Most states, as well as the federal government, provide for the protection of trade secrets that might have to be provided by a company bidding on a government project. Most governments also seek to protect matters of scientific interest that might be misused by the public. The following exemptions from public disclosure, similar to laws in most other states, are from Idaho **9-340-3** and **4**:

(3) Records, maps or other records identifying the location of archaeological or geophysical sites or endangered species, if not already known to the general public.

(4) Archaeological and geologic records concerning exploratory drilling, logging, mining and other excavation, when such records are required to be filed by statute for the time provided by statute.

Most state laws include some provision such as this from Indiana **IC 5-14-3-4(a)**, which makes it illegal to release "documents containing information concerning research, including research conducted under the auspices of an institution of higher learning" and "patient medical records and charts created by a health care provider unless the patient provides written consent for the record's disclosure."

The big snag, of course, is that medical insurance companies have large databanks through which they freely exchange data. Often a person seeking private medical insurance finds that he can acquire medical insurance that covers everything *except* conditions he thinks he will likely encounter in the future. On top of that, recent television news shows have discussed physicians who put unusual, exemplary or baffling cases on the Internet. Although patients' names theoretically are not released on the Internet, it may not be hard for a determined person to find out who they are.

Tennessee, in **49-7-120**, specifically exempts "sponsored research" from disclosure acts. Be aware that science and engineering departments of many universities obtain significantly large proportions of their operating funds from doing research sponsored and paid for by private firms. This money would instantly dry up if the firms had any reason to suspect that their rivals could obtain the same information for no more than a copying cost.

Most states also prohibit the release of information that would identify library patrons and connect them with the material they check out. During the short period of time I worked as a librarian in Salt Lake City, library higher-ups were absolutely horrified when I pointed out in writing that in some situations— to be decided by the head of the library along with the library's attorney of record and *not* by an individual library employee— release of such information might prevent or solve a crime. My comment was considered as incorrect politically as one could possibly be. A few months after the library system decided it could dispense with my services, a shooting occurred in the downtown library. Although I was most dismayed by the nightmarish situation and applauded the courage of library officials and the deputy sheriff involved, I was amused to see on television the next day a librarian telling a television reporter exactly what type of books the criminal involved in the case had recently checked out. Things like this seem to depend on whose ox is gored.

Most states are touchy about who can receive criminal history record information. Virginia Code **§19.2-289** provides:
A. Criminal history record information shall be disseminated, whether directly or through an intermediary, only to:
1. Authorized officers or employees of criminal justice agencies . . .
2. Such other individuals and agencies which require criminal history record information to implement a state or federal statute or executive order . . . .
3. Individuals and agencies pursuant to a specific agreement with a criminal justice agency to provide services required for the administration of criminal justice. . . .

Seventeen more appropriate recipients of this information are listed. Neither private detectives nor amateur detectives are on the list. Does this mean your detective, or your detective's opponent, cannot acquire this information? Dream on. As with library information, it all depends on whose ox is gored, or whose ox is grazing in whose pasture.

Just about any respectable individual, and some individuals who aren't so respectable, can acquire just about any criminal information they want, provided they know one law enforcement officer with enough clout to ask for it. One case involved a woman who had been missing for ten years and whose whereabouts had to be determined to settle a complicated estate. The executor of the estate "caused a search of state and federal arrest records to be made" (private communication, name withheld) by getting a friend of his in a police department to run a records check. As the woman's criminal history was lengthy up until the time she went missing, the executor of the estate intends to appeal to the court that her continued absence from anybody's arrest records, as well as her failure to make any contact in ten years with any member of her family including her children, can be taken as presumptive evidence that the woman is dead.

Virginia's **§2.1-378** has an interesting provision:
B.1. There shall be no personal information system whose existence is secret.

That is, although the personal information contained in the system may be kept secret (rightfully so if it concerns someone's financial, physical or mental health), the existence of the database, in whatever form the database is kept, must be known to the public. Further:

B.8. Any agency holding personal information shall assure its reliability and take precautions to prevent its misuse.

This kind of statute would be wonderful if it were possible to uphold it. But in any agency, at any level, there are always people willing to do a friend a favor, in some cases as an honest act of friendship and in other cases because the "friend" is offering a tidy bribe.

Kansas, in its section **45-221**, provides that any records and statistics more than seventy years old should be open whether or not they are records that would otherwise be closed. Many other jurisdictions have such provisions; the open date may be as short as fifty years or as long as one hundred years. If your amateur is working on a historical case, such laws as these might be useful.

Canada

Canada has simplified its Freedom of Information Act (which is combined with its Privacy Act) by providing a simple form for citizens to fill out. It provides the following information:

Step 1

You (or your detective) must first do enough homework to figure out which government institution is most likely to hold information about you. That will help you decide whether you can safely make an informal request for the information, or whether a formal request is needed. To make an informal request, you would call, write or visit the appropriate institution, using information from *Info Source* (Sources of Federal Government Information) publications, which are available in most major libraries, federal government offices and constituency offices of members of Parliament.

Step 2

If you decide to make a formal application, you will need to complete a form normally available anywhere *Info Source* publications are found. You will need to specify what information you want and provide any details necessary for the institution to locate the information.

The rest of the form is quite simple. You must list the federal government institution believed to hold the information; state whether you wish to examine the information as it is, all in English or all in French; provide details concerning the information; state whether you wish to receive copies of the originals or examine the originals in government offices; state your name, address and telephone number; and sign and date the following statement:

> I request access to personal information about myself under the *Privacy Act* as I am a Canadian citizen, permanent resident or another individual, including an inmate, present in Canada.

If you need help, ask a librarian or staff person with a member of Parliament to help you refer to *Info Source*, which describes the various personal information databases. You may also need to write to the Privacy Coordinator of the agency from which you need information.

Step 3

After you have filled out the request form, you will need to mail or hand-carry it to the Privacy Coordinator of the specific government agency, using its address as it is listed in *Info Source*.

Step 4

When you receive your reply, you need to carefully review it to determine whether it is adequate, or whether you want to make a follow-up request. If you believe you have received inadequate or incomplete information, you may complain to the Privacy Commissioner.

This procedure sounds nice and simple, but if you are not in Canada and have no reason to believe Canada possesses any information about you, or if you want information about somebody or something other than yourself, the situation may get complicated. In real life, you'd probably need to hire a researcher or perhaps an attorney; in fiction, I'd suggest being as vague as possible as to how the information reached the character, unless the method is important to your story. In that case, you're back to hiring a researcher.

But no matter who you hire, the Freedom of Information Act specifically exempts from release much of the information likely to be useful to an amateur detective:

22.(1)The head of a government institution may refuse to disclose any personal information requested under subsection 12(1)

(a) that was obtained or prepared by any government institution, or part of any government institution, that is an investigative body specified in the regulations in the course of lawful investigations pertaining to

(i) the detection, prevention or suppression of crime,

(ii) the enforcement of any law of Canada or a province, or

(iii) activities suspected of constituting threats to the security of Canada within the meaning of the *Canadian Security Intelligence Service Act,*

if the information came into existence less than twenty years prior to the request;

(b) the disclosure of which could reasonably be expected to be injurious to the enforcement of any law of Canada or a province or the conduct of lawful investigations, including, without restricting the generality of the foregoing, any such information

(i) relating to the existence or nature of a particular investigation,

(ii) that would reveal the identity of a confidential source of information, or

(iii) that was obtained or prepared in the course of an investigation; or

(c) the disclosure of which could reasonably be expected to be injurious to the security of penal institutions.

Canada also has become very concerned about some of the invasions of privacy that *are* possible (and which your amateur snoop might find very useful). *The Privacy Commissioner's Annual Report for 1994-1995* (pps. 17-18) contains a number of recommendations that might improve the security of E-mail and other types of electronic communication, which experts now believe will be impossible to either monitor or protect. The report expresses considerable concern about other invasions of privacy:

> In late March, an American company launched a home drug testing kit—"Drug Alert"—targeted at worried parents and suspicious employers.
>
> The kit contains a piece of pre-moistened cloth that can be wiped across doorknobs, desk-tops and clothing to pick up traces of illicit drugs. The cloth is then placed in a sealed envelope and returned for analysis. The company promises to detect the presence of about 30 illegal drugs.
>
> Assuming the testing process is accurate, the information it produces is ambiguous. The test does not confirm that the person used drugs; it merely shows contact with traces of a drug which could be completely innocent. Contact with other drug users could leave a residue sufficient to generate positive test results. Anyone who handles . . . paper money may pick up traces of cocaine, given the bills' frequent use as straws for inhaling the powder.
>
> • • •
>
> The kit is a device for spying on children and a surreptitious invasion of privacy. The consequences of error for parent-child relationships could be fatal. We once feared invasions of privacy by the state, then by the private sector. Must we now fear our own family?

Squidgy-Gate

As this chapter receives its final rewriting, the news is telling us that a new United States federal communications act, replacing the one that has been in place for most of the twentieth century, has just been passed. The provisions of the bill are not yet available, but it is safe to assume that it will carry forward the old and very strict rules against disclosure by a telephone company of anything contained in a telephone conversation. Most other countries have similar rules.

These rules were enforceable when generally nobody

except a telephone company employee would have access to a telephone conversation. Even then, legal or illegal taps by law enforcement officials or criminals were not at all uncommon. Now, at best, these rules can be considered only partially enforceable.

Modern technology, no matter how thoroughly regulated by government, creates unparalleled ability for people to eavesdrop. In almost all countries, governments legally control both the airways and various communications media. But we have all recently seen the spectacle of private telephone calls belonging to the Prince and Princess of Wales being taped, transcribed and released to a very amused world. The Prince was quoted as telling his mistress he wanted to be reincarnated as her Tampax, and the Princess giggled as a lover called her "Squidgy" and gave rather graphic descriptions of what he would like to be doing at the moment. Business calls or crime-related calls, especially but not solely if made on mobile, cellular or cordless phones, are equally vulnerable. All of these calls are actually being broadcast on particular segments of the radio wave spectrum, and if your detective—or your detective's worst enemy—can find the right channel to listen to, the telephone call is no longer secret.

And other concerns arrive that could not have been envisioned twenty years ago. In early 1995, Boston University School of Public Health published a model "Genetic Privacy Act," here summarized by its drafters, in hopes that all governments would adopt it:

> [T]he overarching premise of the act is that no stranger should have or control identifiable DNA samples or genetic information about an individual unless that individual specifically authorizes the collection of DNA samples for the purpose of genetic analysis, authorizes the creation of that private information, and has access to and control over the dissemination of that information.
>
> The rules protecting genetic privacy must be clear and known to the medical, scientific, business and law enforcement communities and the public. The purpose of the Genetic Privacy Act is to codify these rules.
>
> [Quoted in *Privacy Commissioner Report*, p. 21.]

Is this likely to matter to you? Can anybody possibly get your DNA without your knowledge? Think about this: One of the main components of dust is dried-up skin cells. And the cells of all living beings contain DNA. If anybody can get hold of any of your laundry before it is washed, or maybe your hairbrush, toothbrush or washcloth . . . well, there goes your DNA into somebody's laboratory files.

More and more, government privacy acts and information acts will have to address modern biochemistry, modern engineering and the Information Superhighway. Things are possible now that were not possible as recently as ten years ago; ten years from now, things will probably be possible that most of us cannot even imagine. Government control and protection are becoming increasingly difficult to enforce. This may impact your fiction; it *will* impact your life.

All of this means that the strongest right to privacy laws that can possibly be passed, as well as the most generous freedom of information laws, can be no more than relative. As good as their intentions are, as strong as the statute law might become, any of these are enforceable only so far as bureaucrats are willing to enforce them, and/or technology allows them to be enforced. And this situation, in turn, means that your detective, or your detective's opponent, may get or not get just about any information he or she wants. That's why, ultimately, the present laws constitute little more than mythology.

As you study this chapter, remember that *all* governments *always* change their laws. The fact that information is accurate as this book is being written does not mean it is necessarily accurate by the publication date; if it is accurate at the publication date, it may become inaccurate before it reaches you. Unless you are willing to take a chance, *ask first* before you have your detective getting away with doing something that might be illegal or being refused information by a government agency.

HOW REAL AMATEURS SOLVE REAL CASES

The first question here might be, *are* there any real amateur detectives? Are any crimes solved by private citizens? I mentioned to one police officer that I was exploring this matter and asked how many cases he thought were solved by amateurs. He grinned and replied, "Probably a lot more than we think."

Of course, the world is not crawling with real Charlotte Pitts and Lord Peter Wimseys, Mr. and Mrs. Norths and Nick and Nora Charleses. We were unable to discover even *one* amateur detective who has become involved in a series of crimes by accident; we found only two who had done it deliberately. The first is questionably amateur: Erle Stanley Gardner's Court of Last Resort was largely staffed by attorneys and detectives working on their free time, so the few real amateurs involved in it were working under the direction of professionals. Only Princeton, New Jersey's Jim McClosky is a real multicase amateur.

Formerly a successful businessman, he had an unusual midlife crisis. He left his business and enrolled in a seminary.

As a divinity student, he began working in the prison system where he heard bitter tales from inmates who swore they were in prison unjustly.

Most convicts claim that; most of them are lying. But McClosky came to realize that some of them were telling the truth. Determined to help those innocents, he left the seminary and began to formulate his own investigative techniques. He has now been materially instrumental in freeing sixteen people from prison, asking only that they lead productive new lives. Part PI, part lay priest, McClosky is still at work righting wrongs. (From a CBS Evening News report.)

But newspapers, magazines and books frequently report individual amateur involvement in, and solution of, real crimes. These determined people—and I chose that adjective carefully, because determination is a far more important element of their character than brilliance—tend to fall into several clear categories.

The Personally Involved Amateur

The first category includes people who are victims of crimes or are falsely accused, and their friends and relations. In 1995, Ohio newspapers reported the seventeen years of work done by Ray Callihan to prove not only that his daughter was murdered, but also who probably killed her. When Sharon, only nineteen, was found dead in a field in 1978, the coroner ruled her death the result of the often-deadly combination of Valium and alcohol. The bruised fingermarks on her neck were completely ignored.

Callihan spent sixteen years and thousands of dollars on the case, but it wasn't until 1994, when reporter Alisa Lenhoff of the Warren, Ohio, *Tribune Chronicle* became involved, that an exhumation order was issued. An autopsy determined that Sharon had indeed been strangled. Her former boyfriend, Robert Burns, whom Callihan had suspected from the start, was charged with the murder. At this time, trial results are pending.

Both parents of a rape victim in Columbus, Ohio, planned the strategy that led to the arrest of Robert Biddings, who was ultimately found guilty of forty counts of rape, kidnapping and aggravated robbery and who would later plead guilty to another seventy-three counts. After one of the victims was assaulted in June 1987, her parents determined to catch the man whether or not the police could. For nearly a year, they grimly stayed in the area of the rape during the hours when the rapist was known to strike, the attractive mother making herself a decoy while the father watched from hiding. Just over a year later, Biddings attacked the woman. He was holding a gun to her head when the woman's husband burst out of hiding with his own pistol. Biddings, panicked by the unexpected defense, ran, but the amateur detectives got his automobile license number and police arrested him shortly thereafter. The story that unfolded then was one of a horrifyingly long series of crimes. The man is already sentenced to prison for a time somewhat longer than the life of Methuselah, and at least one more state is ready to extradite him if he is ever paroled. If the Biddings hadn't come up with their plan, there is no guessing how long the man might have continued his spree of destruction.

Sometimes the brilliant amateur is the victim of the crime. In Johannesburg, South Africa, a twenty-six-year-old secretary set out to catch the man who had raped her. After police tried and failed to identify the rapist, the victim took the daring step of placing the following advertisement in the local newspaper:

TO THE MAN WHO RAPED ME FEB. 4:

I've known men before, but never anyone like you. Your love was strong, exciting, addictive. Ever since that night in my apartment on Fourth Street I have been unable to get you out of my mind. This is a plea to you, my rough lover: I want you to come back. I want you in my arms again. My number is XXX-XXXX. I'll be waiting for your call.

Incredibly, rapist Patrick O'Connor responded by telephoning her. The victim, shaking in terror, kept her head long enough to make a date for the next night. Then she immediately called the police to tell them what she had done.

Police, fearing that the rapist might show up early for the date, set up round-the-clock protection. When the rapist showed up right on schedule, the three officers remained in hiding long enough to tape-record a discussion between the criminal and his victim about the rape the month before. Faced in court with that evidence, O'Connor plead guilty and was sentenced to fifteen years in prison.

Not all amateur detective work concerns major cases. Joyce Johnson of Roy, Utah, cried herself to sleep after the second time her house was burglarized. Awaking later in a total rage, she set herself to locating the burglars. In the first burglary, the burglars had called the house to be sure no one was home; not realizing the answering machine was running, they conversed with each other. Mrs. Johnson's sons thought they recognized one of the voices as that of a former houseguest. The family turned the tape and name over to the police department, but police decided there was insufficient evidence for arrest. The second time the burglars struck, a stolen suitcase with identification still on it turned up in the trash receptacle of a nearby retail store. Mrs. Johnson searched through the large trash receptacles of every store in the area, finding nothing else. She then started checking pawnbrokers in Roy and in a gradually widening area, which eventually took in two counties. She finally located her CD player in a pawnshop, pawned in the name of the suspect in the first burglary. More of her stolen property turned up in secondhand stores. This time the police made an arrest; the first suspect confessed and pleaded guilty to one second-degree felony, but the second suspect has not been located.

So Mrs. Johnson won? Well . . . not quite. Much of her property, including over $5,000 worth of heirloom jewelry, is still missing; and the $8,000 in restitution the suspect has been ordered to pay will not replace the sentiment.

In January 1995, an Ogden, Utah, couple was quite distressed when their thirteen-year-old daughter told them that she and a friend had been followed home from school. The man had repeatedly driven up beside them, opened his car door and exposed his genitals to them. At one time, he drove into a store parking lot the girls had to cross, opened his car door and gestured for the girls to approach him as he displayed himself.

The girls got a partial license plate number, but when parents called the police to describe the car and provide what information they had, they were told that it would take quite a while

---

Victim Privacy

In all real rape cases, we have made it a policy to omit all names and other identifying detail. In some parts of the United States, disclosure in print of a rape victim's name is forbidden by law; it should remain a matter of policy until the day is reached when the victim of a crime is no longer blamed for the crime by large segments of the population.

---

to check all the possibilities. The mother was rather disgusted by that response. The girls had all except the last letter of the license plate, and it was obvious that the total number of possibilities amounted to a maximum of twenty-six. As she had access to license plate records through her work for the state, she went and made the identification herself. The father then confronted the suspect at his home before notifying police that the identification had been made. The suspect fled, but later surrendered to officers and confessed that he had been exposing himself to children for some time.

Minor crime? Yes. But the immediacy of his capture might prevent a major crime later. (However, police strongly recommend that amateurs, no matter how brilliant or closely related to the victim they might be, should *never* confront suspects—especially alone.)

Susan Billig became an amateur detective one sunny afternoon in March 1974. That was the day her seventeen-year-old daughter, Amy, disappeared without a trace.

Amy would be thirty-eight years old today, but her whereabouts still remains a mystery. She was last seen leaving her parents' house in Coconut Grove, Florida, to make the one-mile trip to her father's art gallery. Her mother believed she was abducted by a motorcycle gang that was headed to the races in Daytona Beach, but there was not enough information for the police to use.

In 1976, Susan and her husband went to Tulsa after reports from a biker that Amy was the girlfriend of one of his pals, but the biker vanished before the parents arrived in Oklahoma. In 1978, Susan received a report from a lawyer in New Jersey that Amy was with bikers there. A third witness said that a local mechanic who worked on his disabled car in Ocala, Florida, claimed he'd taken the "missing teen from Coconut Grove." That clue went nowhere because local police mislaid the visiting motorist's report and couldn't locate the mechanic's name.

One biker gang in Seattle actually offered to help Susan find her daughter and, if possible, reclaim her from rival bikers. But that effort, too, proved fruitless, as did countless other reports of Amy wandering the streets of various cities with biker gangs.

Even after her husband, Ned, died recently, Susan Billig kept searching around the country for her daughter. Before her husband's death, she even joined a biker gang in hopes of learning Amy's location. The gang told the sleuthing mom that they had seen her teenaged daughter riding with a rival outfit, but Susan always seemed to be one step behind.

The twenty-year search cost the Billigs their life savings, art gallery and home. Not only have they gone through the trauma of the search, but they also had to endure countless harassing telephone calls from a man who claimed he was the kidnapper. Over the years, the self-proclaimed kidnapper would call the Billigs and describe in lurid detail what he had done to Amy, including selling her into forced prostitution and cutting out her tongue so that she couldn't talk.

The man whom the police and FBI finally arrested for the telephone calls turned out to be a highly decorated, twenty-four-year veteran of the Customs Service, responsible for drug interdiction at the Port of Miami. But disappointingly, all evidence indicated that he was *not* responsible for Amy's disappearance.

Despite this arrest, the FBI and a senior Miami detective who has worked on the case for years are still frustrated as the arrest has not resulted in locating Amy Billig and solving one of the most puzzling crimes of the century.

And Susan Billig? The plucky widow will keep on sleuthing until she dies. She's hoping her daughter is as much a survivor as she is; or, if Amy's dead, she wants to be able to bury her.

The story of Tommy Burkett has been shown on *Unsolved Mysteries* numerous times and remains one of the most controversial crimes and alleged cover-ups in Northern Virginia.

Young Tommy's parents, Tom Burkett and Beth (Burkett) George, turned relentless amateur sleuths to get the facts on what really happened the day their son was murdered. Here are the facts alleged by *Unsolved Mysteries* to be accurate:

Tommy was a twenty-one-year-old student in his junior year at Marymount University in Arlington, Virginia, when he was murdered on December 1, 1991. Tommy not only worked part time at the University's admissions office, but also worked undercover for the U.S. Drug Enforcement Administration (DEA) and had reported drug-dealing activities.

His parents allege that a conspiracy ensued between the local police, medical examiner and Commonwealth's attorney. Why? Because one of the alleged killers was a Marymount student whose father was a DEA agent, and his alleged accomplice was the grandson of one of the university's trustees. Sound complicated and complex? It is. Here are some of the facts and extraordinary amateur sleuthing done by Burkett's parents.

Tommy's badly beaten body was found in his room by his parents at 6:12 P.M. on December 1. They immediately called fire and rescue, whose personnel arrived in minutes and verified that Tommy had been dead for hours. When the police arrived, the investigating officer insisted that the crime had only just happened, probably while the parents were walking up the driveway, and recorded the time of injury at 6:10 P.M. and the time of death at 7:30 P.M.—despite the fact that Tommy's body was removed from the house a few minutes after 7:00 P.M. by the police department.

The police left behind the following evidence: bullets in the wall, several hundred bloodstains that were both upstairs and downstairs, and an unsigned note dated July 19th that was handprinted in block letters stating, "I want to be cremated." It was this note, not even in Tommy's handwriting, that the police labeled a suicide note. They also discarded Tommy's bloody clothes without informing his parents, who called this an attempt to destroy evidence.

The autopsy report failed to note obvious bodily injuries, and the medical examiner did not visit the crime scene. When the parents questioned the report, the medical examiner showed them photos of the injuries; but those photos were later missing from the files. The examiner's report was issued the day after the body was found, before the autopsy had even been done. The police investigator refused to take fingerprints from the crime scene, remove the bullet from the wall, interview neighbors, or investigate missing personal items from the house and the presence of strange cars at the house at the time of Tommy's death. The police also could not explain, and wouldn't investigate, the question of how Tommy's missing car mysteriously returned later.

The parents contacted the Commonwealth attorney for help. There they encountered more problems. In a newspaper interview, the attorney rejected all of the parents' claims but would not respond to or return their phone calls and letters. The parents then requested information and files on their son's case through the Freedom of Information Act, but their request was denied by the Commonwealth attorney. When the parents complained to Virginia's attorney general, they were reportedly called "vipers" by the Commonwealth attorney in a newspaper article.

Where does the Burkett case stand today? The story can be seen on cable TV's *Unsolved Mysteries*. The parents have formed a group called "Parents Against Corruption & Coverup" and publish a newsletter called *The Bulldog*, which reports their continuing efforts to bring to justice the killer or killers of their son. They hired their own medical examiner and arranged for exhumation; that second autopsy directly contradicted the Fairfax County medical examiner's conclusion that Tommy Burkett had committed suicide. They also had a private ballistic report done on the bullet in the bedroom wall; that report contradicted the county medical examiner's report that this was the fatal bullet, a report that was made despite the fact that police never dug the bullet out of the wall. One police officer complained to the Burketts that the Feds told them how to handle the case. The death of Tommy Burkett may be a closed file to the police, but Beth George and Tom Burkett, who continue fighting for the truth, still have not washed their son's blood off the walls of the house in Herndon, Virginia.

The Noninvolved Amateur

The second category of amateur detective, also illustrated in the Callihan case, is the uninvolved person who becomes curious.

As in that case, he or she is likely to be a reporter. According to Jay Nash (author of *The Encyclopedia of World Crime*), it was "Isaac 'Ike' White, of the New York *World*" who became very curious about the death of Annie Buchanan in 1892. Originally believed to have died of a stroke, Mrs. Buchanan was buried quietly. Nobody except James Smith, the janitor of the whorehouse the victim's husband frequented, questioned the decision. But when White, who apparently frequented the same whorehouse, heard the janitor muttering "Buchanan murdered her just the same, to get her money, I know it," White started asking questions.

Prowling around, White discovered that the unfortunate woman's husband, Dr. Robert Buchanan, had told bartender Michael Macomber that Annie was threatening suicide. He learned that Dr. Buchanan had cancelled a proposed trip to London, telling the steamship company there had been a death in the family, *before* Annie died. He also learned that Buchanan had been very interested when medical student Carlyle Harris was convicted of murdering his wife by poisoning her with morphine, a crime revealed when medical examiners noticed the pupils of her eyes contracted to the size of pinpoints. Buchanan bragged to Macomber that he knew a way Harris could have avoided getting caught: he should have mixed atropine with the morphine or used atropine eyedrops just before she succumbed, as the atropine would have counteracted the effect of the morphine on the eyes.

Armed with that information, White went to the police. The trial, long and complicated, involved a tremendous amount of expert testimony, and Buchanan was ultimately convicted. He was executed July 2, 1895.

It has been said that "the perfect crime" is the one nobody ever suspects was committed. If it hadn't been for the angry janitor and interested reporter, Buchanan's would have been the perfect crime . . . maybe. Perhaps he should have tipped the janitor, but tipping the janitor didn't work forty-odd years earlier in Massachusetts.

It was another janitor who directed attention the right way after the famous disappearance in 1849 of Dr. George Parkman, a faculty member of what later became the Harvard Medical

The Perfect Crime

Have any perfect crimes ever been committed? Probably far more than anyone ever suspects. Poison is the easiest method. Several times a year, the news tells us of someone arrested for poisoning; usually it isn't until ten or more people bite the dust that poison is even suspected. If such a person stopped on one or two, he or she would certainly get away with it; in many of these cases, *nobody except an amateur (at least an amateur in terms of law enforcement)* would ever be in a position to notice problems. Bank fraud and stock fraud are equally easy crimes to commit and equally likely to go unsuspected.

School. Police sought high and low; ironically, faculty member Dr. John W. Webster, tried to "help." He told police he was probably the last person to see Parkman alive when he repaid about $500 of a loan Parkman had made him. He suggested the money as the motive for a robbery-murderer.

But janitor Ephraim Littlefield was not satisfied with that explanation. He knew, even if the police didn't, that there had been bad blood between Parkman and Webster. He knew that the wall behind Webster's assay oven had been very hot the day after Parkman's disappearance. When Webster, a notorious tightwad, presented Littlefield a Thanksgiving turkey, Littlefield rightly read the gesture as a bribe. A few days later, using a pry bar, he removed some bricks from the assay oven and found human bones there, including a pelvis and some legbones. When he summoned police, they made a further search and found Parkman's teeth in the oven. Despite the identification of the teeth by Parkman's dentist, Webster continued to insist he'd only burned a used-up cadaver.

The trial was dramatic with defense lawyers inquiring whether anybody *really* wanted to take the word of a janitor over the word of an eminent professor. But the teeth told their own story. Webster was hanged on August 30, 1850. Long after the trial and shortly before the hanging, he admitted the murder.

In a case broadcast on CBS news on February 26, 1996,

Dr. John Hall of Michigan's Albion College was surprised to find himself an amateur detective. A collector of World War I aircraft memorabilia, Hall had been astonished to find an unusually fine airplane nosepiece for sale. It had been built for a German fighter plane and then, after crashing once, was rebuilt and repainted for the use of an American fighter plane. Try as he might, Hall absolutely could not think of any possible source for this nosepiece other than the Smithsonian Institution. He took his suspicions to the FBI.

At FBI request, Hall agreed to purchase the nosepiece and ask for more memorabilia that was as good. To his astonishment as well as that of the FBI, the seller—Carl Schneide, who was a Smithsonian employee—replied to Hall *on Smithsonian letterhead*. He invited Hall to pick out what he wanted from the museum with the agreement that Schneide would then secretly remove the items and turn them over to Hall for a reasonable fee. Hall was wired for sound, and FBI agents listened as deals were made. When arrested, Schneide pled guilty; he did only six months' time for his thefts from "the nation's attic."

The Psychic Gets Involved

The third category of real amateurs is the interesting and broad one of psychics, some of them professional psychics but more of them one-shot psychics who have "seen" the events of only one case. This category sometimes overlaps with the first. Perhaps the best-known case, often called *The Murder in the Red Barn* (the name of the play based on it), is the death of Maria Marten in Polstead, England, in 1827. That spring Maria left home with her lover William Corder, ostensibly to be married in Ipswich. The elopement was encouraged by her parents since Maria had already given birth to Corder's stillborn baby. However, it had to be kept secret because, Corder insisted, he would be in trouble if his mother heard he was to marry a woman who had given birth to a bastard (even if it *was* his). He ordered Maria to meet him in a red-tiled barn on his property, wearing male clothes with her own clothing hidden in a bag. The marriage seemed at first to be legitimate, but for the next ten months nobody heard from Maria. Corder, in his frequent visits to his mother's farm in Polstead, always assured everyone that Maria was well and happy. Sometimes she was in London; sometimes she was in Yarmouth; sometimes she was in France. There was always some good reason why she couldn't visit this time, and *of course* she'd come along next time.

In most cases, such assurances, from a landed man to a peasant couple, would be accepted without question. But Maria could write. And her ongoing invisibility, along with the nonreceipt of letters, began to arouse questions among the family. Maria's stepbrother also reported seeing Corder carrying a shovel and pickax to the barn the same day Maria vanished.

Maria's stepmother, who was having nightmares, would dream over and over that Maria came to her, insisting that Corder had murdered her and buried her body in the red-tiled barn on the Corder farm. Mrs. Marten at first dismissed the dreams; *of course* Maria was married and happy. She was probably just too busy to write. Maybe she was with child, or had a new baby to care for.

But the dreams continued, and Mrs. Marten continued to report them to her husband. Finally, in order to stop her nagging, Maria's father agreed to investigate. He went to the barn with a friend and found the floor littered with what seemed like tons of debris. After beginning to move the debris, the two men came upon a patch of dirt that seemed loose. They began to dig. Fred Archer, in *Crime in the Psychic World* (p.49), says that they "found that the earth was, in truth, unexpectedly loose under the spades." After digging no more than eighteen inches, they came upon rough sacking. When they continued to dig around and through the sacking, they came upon Maria's green silk handkerchief—a gift from Corder.

Below the sacking and the handkerchief was the decaying body of Maria. Corder admitted burying her but insisted he hadn't killed her; rather, she had stolen a pistol from him and shot herself to death. The story might have been a good one, but it wasn't good enough in the face of all the evidence. Ultimately Corder was convicted of seducing, impregnating and then murdering Maria Marten, and was hanged on August 11, 1828. If the stepmother hadn't had her dreams, Corder probably would never have been suspected.

The Ones Who Got Away . . .

On at least one occasion, the alleged victim cleared his murderer after the psychic "brilliant amateur" proved to be not very brilliant or psychic at all. The case began with the same sort of dreams as those that identified the murderer of Maria Marten. Russel Colvin vanished from Manchester, Vermont, in May of 1812, leaving behind his wife Sally just days after having a quarrel with her brothers Stephen and Jesse Boorn. Colvin had vanished before for weeks at a time, so at first nobody thought anything of it. But in the spring of 1819 Sally's uncle, Amos Boorn, dreamed about Colvin's ghost. He reported to police that he had dreamed three times about the ghost, and each time the ghost had told him he was buried in the remains of a burned silo on Uncle Amos's land.

Police ignored him until a few days later when bones were discovered near the reported location of the burial. Despite the fact that the bones turned out to be those of an animal, the brothers were convicted of murder on the sworn testimony of a known forger. This man stated that Jesse had admitted to him that Stephen killed Colvin and Jesse had helped with the burial. The purported murderer was sentenced to be hanged, and his brother was sentenced to life in prison.

Close to the time Stephen was to die, one James Whelpley read in a New York newspaper about the case and brought it to the attention of Colvin, whom he knew. Quite astonished, Colvin returned to Manchester to appear before the court and point out that as he was still alive, his brothers-in-law could not possibly have murdered him.

The "murderers" were released, and Colvin departed once more, this time for good.

Cases like this may explain why psychics are usually, though not always, ignored by police. Such was the case when the remains of Donna Macho were discovered near East Windsor, New Jersey, five years after psychic John Monti told police where they were. After part of the area was examined without results, police called off the search, only to be embarrassed five years later when a Boy Scout leader stumbled upon the missing woman's skeleton—in the same soybean field where Monti had claimed the body lay.

... and the Ones Who Didn't

In cases without psychic involvement, sometimes the "brilliant amateur" is neither so brilliant, nor such an amateur. Jay Nash tells the story of Jean Burrows, a British journalist found floating in three feet of water in a millionaires' yacht basin in Bermuda. Last seen heading back to her hotel by moped after dinner at a restaurant, the twenty-four-year-old woman had been raped, knocked unconscious and then drowned. Bermuda police, baffled by the case, eventually asked for help from Scotland Yard. Inspectors William Wright and Basil Haddrell, arriving and proceeding with the investigation by sending physical evidence to London for analysis and then conducting a house-to-house investigation, eventually developed a suspect. But they were faced by that age-old dilemma of investigators: I know who did it, but can I prove it?

On inviting the suspect, Paul Augustus Belvin, to visit them at the police station, they discovered him to be knowledgeable about the area and the local gossip. He indicated that he was very clever and eager to help the police. Wright, who had a pretty good idea of what was going on, surprised Haddrell, his superior, by asking Belvin if he would like to be an amateur detective and assist them in the investigation. Belvin eagerly agreed. He then proceeded to act out the entire crime in accurate and precise detail, even leading the detectives to the murder weapon, an iron pipe he had thrown into the sea. Tests on Belvin's clothing proved conclusively that he was the murderer. On September 1, 1971, he confessed.

Belvin eventually was sentenced to life in prison. This serves as a good warning to any murderer who tries to get too smart (*The Enclycopedia of World Crime*, p. 322).

Sometimes there isn't any real question who committed the crime. Like professionals in a similar situation, the amateur, rather than identify the criminal, must force the legal system to take appropriate action. Such was the case of Clover Forsythe of Gouverneur, New Jersey. Five men who had raped her sister were allowed to plead guilty to "sexual misconduct" (a misdemeanor rather than a felony) and were ordered to pay a $750 fine and a $90 surcharge each. Forsythe, speaking in the November 1994 issue of *McCall's*, described the judge as preceding the sentence

What kind of murders do women commit? Historically, women have been most likely to commit infanticide (by smothering, drowning, or abandoning the unwanted baby), poisoning (because women prepare the food in most places, which makes poisoning easier for women than for men), and—surprisingly—ax murders. Psychologists believe that the reason for the ferocity of the ax murderer, who almost never stops with one blow, is fear: the murderer has always felt, rightly or wrongly, that society has disempowered her, that her victim is a part of that society and, therefore, that unless she strikes so many blows the victim is reduced to a shapeless mass of blood, bone, and brains, the victim is likely to jump up and attack her.

by saying, "This is the toughest sentence my court has ever had to impose." Apparently in his mind, the fact that the victim had been drunk at the time of the assault reduced the criminality of gang rape.

Forsythe, enraged by the situation, led a campaign to force the state to abandon the plea bargain and recharge the men with rape. In February 1994, the governor ordered the state attorney general to reopen the case; in March, the attorney general did so; and in April, the judge ruled that the men would be charged with rape. The case continues.

And the Writers Enter the Case

The final important category is that of writers, often mystery writers. Yes, mystery writers frequently solve real mysteries. Sometimes these are classic cases such as that of Lizzie Borden, which has been "solved" in many ways by various writers over the years. But occasionally they are current cases that must be solved correctly and quickly to prevent a miscarriage of justice.

The first such case—and it had to be the first because Edgar Allan Poe is frequently called "the father of the detective story"—is the death of Mary Cecilia Rogers in New York in July of 1841, a case that Poe immortalized a year later as "The

---

A Case Immortalized by Poe

"... 'There was evidence,' it is said, 'of a struggle. ... The pieces of the frock torn out by the bushes were about three inches wide and six inches long.... They *looked like strips torn off.*' Here, inadvertently, *Le Soleil* [actually the Philadelphia *Saturday Evening Post*] has employed an exceedingly suspicious phrase. The pieces, as described, do indeed 'look like strips torn off'; but purposely and by hand. It is one of the rarest of accidents that a piece is 'torn off,' from any garment such as is now in question, by the agency of *a thorn.* From the very nature of such fabrics, a thorn or nail becoming tangled in them, tears them rectangularly—divides them into two longitudinal rents, at right angles with each other, and meeting at an apex where the thorn enters—but it is scarcely possible to conceive the piece 'torn off.' ... To tear a piece *off* from such fabric, two distinct forces, in different directions, will be, in almost every case, required. ..."

—*"The Mystery of Marie Rogêt"*

Mystery of Marie Rogêt." Although Poe translated the victim's name and moved the scene to Paris, his reconstruction of the case was considered by many to be quite accurate. (At least as many others considered it wildly inaccurate, despite the fact that in later years Poe's publishers included with the story their insistence that Poe's reconstruction had been borne out by two confessions—of which the entire law enforcement community was apparently quite unaware.)

Mary Rogers was a clerk in a tobacco shop. She was very free with her smiles; she might or might not have been free with other aspects of her person. Mary left her mother's house on Nassau Street on Sunday, July 25th, apparently to visit her sister, whom she never reached. Her body was found floating in the Hudson River on July 28th. The autopsy suggested that she had been repeatedly raped and then immediately strangled. However many people argued that the autopsy was poorly done and what the coroner mistook for evidence of violent sexual assault was actually evidence of an illegal and botched abortion. The fact

Upon the original publication of "Marie Rogêt," the foot-notes here appended were considered unnecessary; but the lapse of several years since the tragedy upon which the tale is based, renders it expedient to give them. . . . A young girl, *Mary Cecilia Rogers*, was murdered in the vicinity of New York; and although her death occasioned an intense and long-enduring excitement, the mystery attending it had remained unsolved at the period when the present paper was written and published (November, 1842). Herein, under pretence of relating the fate of a Parisian *grisette*, the author has followed, in minute detail, the essential, while merely paralleling the inessential, facts of the real murder of Mary Rogers. . . .

. . . It might not be improper to record . . . that the confes-sions of two persons (one of them the Madame Deluc of the narrative), made, at different periods, long subsequent to the publication, confirmed, in full, not only the general conclu-sion but absolutely *all* the chief hypothetical details by which that conclusion was attained.

—comment by original publisher of the story

that the murder apparently took place in New York but the body was found in New Jersey complicated the whole thing. Each jurisdiction attempted to turn the entire case over to the other jurisdiction, and neither jurisdiction had anything approaching a trained professional police force. The one possible suspect, a married man, was cleared by the legal statement of the young woman he had been with, upon whom he had tried unsuccess-fully to force himself.

In Poe's version of the case, that suspect (a Navy officer) was guilty, and had committed the murder, not in the woods where some of the possessions of the victim were discovered, but rather in a seedy cafe owned by one Madame Deluc. Whether or not Poe's reconstruction was accurate—which ap-parently, at least in part, it was not—it is clear that some of Poe's reasoning, put into the mouth of his detective, Chevalier Auguste Dupin, was brilliant. (See sidebar above.)

In 1914, Mary Roberts Rinehart wrote the novel, *The After*

House, a Poe-like reconstruction of the murder of a Navy captain, his wife and another seaman. It was so convincing to President Woodrow Wilson that it resulted in the pardon of First Mate Thomas Mead Bram, who had been convicted of the murder and had served nineteen years in federal prison. Former President Theodore Roosevelt had brought the murder to Wilson's attention and urged the pardon; criminologists now tend to believe that Rinehart was mistaken and Bram was indeed guilty.

Some Classic Cases

Let's return now to the category of brilliant amateur that for most of us is, perhaps, the most interesting. They are the writers who tackle classic cases rather than currently pending ones. Probably the two cases most frequently reworked are the murder of Lizzie Borden's father and stepmother, and the Jack the Ripper murders.

In the case of Lizzie Borden, I have read books "conclusively" proving that Lizzie was guilty, that she was innocent, that her sister (who was known to have been in another town at the time of the murder) was guilty, that an unknown insane illegitimate brother of Lizzie was the murderer, and that Lizzie didn't do it but it's impossible to prove who did. My own conclusion continues to be that Lizzie committed the murders; all the same, she walked.

In the case of Jack the Ripper, theories abound. They range from the reasonably sensible to the unspeakably bizarre. Fred Archer, in *Crime and the Psychic World* (pp. 22-23), insists that psychic medium Robert James Lees' well-known "visions" of the murder were accurate, despite other sources that indicate he fingered an extremely unlikely target: Sir William Gull, one of the best-known physicians in England. Archer goes on to relate a story told by criminologist Harold Dearden.

Dearden said that in 1918, in a dugout on the Somme, a companion (son of a physician who managed a mental asylum outside of London), facetiously mentioned to him that this, his fortieth birthday, was the second of his birthdays to be ruined by others: "his tenth birthday also had been ruined—by Jack the Ripper."

Supposedly, the boy had been promised a birthday trip to the theater, but the trip was cancelled at the last moment by the admission of a new patient with whom the boy later became well acquainted. Only after his father's death, when he was living abroad with an uncle, did the young man ask the cause of the patient's admission to the hospital. He was horrified to be told the patient was Jack the Ripper. He never told Dearden the patient's name. But see the sidebar below for the few things he did tell—none of which point to Gull.

The patient was the son of one of his father's oldest friends. It is a fair assumption that the majority of his father's old friends belonged to his own class, that many would be medical colleagues whose sons were likely (more so in Victorian England than today) to have followed the same profession.

The patient was ambidextrous. So was Jack the Ripper, in the opinion of experts who saw his handiwork.

The boy's tenth birthday fell on November 9, 1888. Jack the Ripper had given his uniquely dramatic farewell performance the night before. And, publicly, was never to be heard from again.

Was There Even a Crime to Solve?

Very often a writer will tackle a case that was not even suspected to be murder, or was suspected in such a way that the suspicions were dismissed by everyone else.

In one of the most interesting books I have ever read, Ben Weider and David Hapgood, working with Dr. Sten Forshufvud, a Swedish toxicologist, investigated the death of Napoleon Bonaparte. For over a hundred and fifty years, many French crime fans have insisted that Napoleon was poisoned by the English while in their custody on the Island of St. Helena. English crime fans have continued to insist that Napoleon died of stomach cancer. The evidence is now in, and no possible doubt remains: Napoleon was murdered with arsenic.

Who did it? Was it the English as so many Frenchmen had claimed?

After the means of death was proven, many people offered, and many other people refused to accept, evidence that suggested the arsenic fell into Napoleon's food from the ceiling, where it had been used on paint and wallpaper, or from the draperies, which were usually dusty. But arsenic can tell its own tale: It leaves traces in the hair, and it remains there permanently *but only in the parts of the hair shaft that were actively growing at the time it was ingested.* Furthermore, the amount of deposition in any given part of the hair is proportional to the amount of arsenic ingested. If its deposition in a hair is not uniform, then the person was being poisoned repeatedly, at separate times, rather than at a uniform rate as would be indicated if the arsenic was in the full length of the hair strand. Scientists can compare the places on a shaft of hair that do contain arsenic with those that do not, ascertain when that strand of hair was cut, and compute the speed with which the hair grew. Armed with that information, they can determine approximately, and often almost exactly, when the arsenic was ingested.

Working with several locks cut from Napoleon's hair immediately after his death and scattered around the world as heirlooms, the authors and toxicologist were able to show that Napoleon ingested fairly large doses of arsenic on or about September 18th through the 21st of 1820, "the tenth to the eighteenth of October, the twenty-fifth of October to the first of November, the twenty-eighth to the thirtieth of December, the twenty-sixth to the twenty-ninth of January [of 1821]; and the twenty-sixth and twenty-seventh of February. In the intervals between those acute attacks he continued to show the symptoms of chronic poisoning." (*The Murder of Napoleon*, p. 139) (The chronic poisoning would be the result of some of the arsenic from each dose settling in the fatty tissue of the body, from which it would later be released as the deposed emperor, now mortally ill, continued to lose weight.) The final, massive dose was apparently administered in mid-April; Napoleon died on May 5th after weeks of vomiting, diarrhea and neurological unpleasantness.

And the murderer? No, he wasn't English. The authors' investigation made it clear that the only person who could possibly have committed the murder was Count Charles-Tristan de Montholon. He was a surviving member of the old French aristocracy who had accompanied Napoleon not to Waterloo but to St. Helena, where his wife Albine apparently became Napoleon's mistress. Montholon, who had charge of the former emperor's wine cellar, is believed to have put the arsenic into Napoleon's personal wine, an unusual vintage not many people liked. On the few occasions when Napoleon presented bottles of the wine to friends they, too, showed signs of the illness that was devouring him, whereas frequent guests in his quarters, including his English warder's young daughter, showed no such signs, which they would have shown if the arsenic had been in the wallpaper or draperies.

Since reading *The Murder of Napoleon*, I have read and heard some arguments against the conclusion that the book draws. I find those arguments unfounded. I, at least, would vote to convict the count.

Another book investigating murder where none was seriously suspected is *In God's Name: An Investigation Into the Murder of Pope John Paul I* by David A. Yallop. In a very well-researched but ultimately unconvincing book, Yallop presents this thesis: Albino Luciani, Pope John Paul I, was murdered by six men who saw their careers crumbling because, during his mere thirty-three days in office, this new Pope had already begun to create reforms that would have blown open the Vatican banking scandal far earlier than it actually did break. The book jacket (see the sidebar) sums up part of Yallop's comments.

Was the Pope murdered? Enough people believed Yallop for the book to become an Alternate Selection of The Book of the Month Club. Enough people disbelieved Yallop that no official steps were taken in response to his book. You be the judge.

The Airman and the Carpenter

Sometimes writers perform their own investigations in attempts to disprove things that have long been "known." It has, for example, long been known that Bruno Hauptmann kidnapped and murdered the small son of famous pilot Charles A. Lindbergh. Hauptmann was tried, convicted and executed and

The Death of Pope John Paul I

Pope John Paul I had, by the evening of September 28, 1978, decided on . . . changes that would affect the doctrine, finances and hierarchy of the . . . Church. These changes would be opposed by . . . six powerful men who knew that the Pope's decisions could mean the end of their careers, if not their lives. Unless, of course, they acted first.

Early on the morning of September 29, Albino Luciani was found dead.

No official death certificate has ever been issued.

No autopsy was performed.

The cause of death, referred to by the Vatican in the vague terms, "possibly related to myocardial infarction," *in fact* remains unknown.

—*book jacket,* In God's Name: An Investigation Into the Murder of Pope John Paul I

fifty years later, in his book *The Airman and the Carpenter,* writer Ludovic Kennedy set forth to prove that Hauptmann was innocent.

Up until now, *The Hand of Hauptmann* and *Kidnap: The Story of the Lindbergh Kidnap Case* were the only books I had read on the subject, and they left me firmly convinced that Hauptmann was guilty. But Kennedy raised a lot of questions in my mind by exploring some of the factors on the basis of which Hauptmann was convicted. If his statements (never mind his interpretations) of the case are accurate, then Hauptmann could not possibly have been guilty. (Hauptmann's one-time business partner Fisch, who inadvertently set him up, was certainly involved, but probably only in money laundering after the fact.)

But there is an extremely disquieting subtext that Kennedy never makes explicit, and which is in the subtext only for people who have a considerable quantity of built-in suspicion (though I believe Kennedy put it there deliberately). It is this:

Who, among all the people involved with the case other

than the mother, grandmother and employees, knew the baby was even in the house that night? (It was the only time he had ever been in that particular house on a Tuesday night.)

Who could have lifted the baby out of his crib and out the window without the baby crying? (The child was not a helpless infant, but a toddler, already walking and talking. Suffering at the time from a bad cold, which made him cranky, he would be that much more likely to awaken on being disturbed and start howling loudly enough to wake everyone in the house.)

Who had a history of springing cruel practical jokes on friends and family?

Who was unskilled enough at carpentry, but knowledge-able enough about mechanics, to have cobbled up the ladder that was used?

Who was cool enough under pressure to keep the secret the rest of his life?

Who was tall enough to use a ladder with sixteen- to eighteen-inch spacing between the rungs instead of the normal twelve?

Who was the only person who claimed to hear the sound that later turned out to be, apparently, the ladder cracking and letting the boy fall to his death, at a time when he was with other people and couldn't possibly have been on the ladder?

The answer, every time, is Charles Lindbergh.

Could Lindbergh have set up a fake kidnapping as a practical joke on his wife? Did the joke turn tragically wrong when the rung of the ladder snapped, and the baby fell to his death? Did Lindbergh bury his own baby near the turnpike, keeping out the sleeping suit to use later to keep the ransom messages going when a living child could not possibly be produced? Did Lindbergh change his testimony not because police had convinced him they were right, but because he had cold-bloodedly decided to sacrifice Hauptmann?

Most of us find such an allegation, aimed at a national hero, repugnant; that's probably why Kennedy was no more open in the allegation than he was. Most of us find the concept of high Vatican leaders conspiring to murder a Pope to be repugnant (though it has certainly happened in the past). But a fact does not become untrue because it is repugnant. The question, therefore, must be one not of whether it is repugnant, but of whether it is true.

Who is right? As with the story of Pope John Paul I, you be the judge. If I were in the jury, we'd probably have a hung jury. No matter who the culprit was in the Lindbergh case, sufficient doubt has been raised in my mind that because of the unavailability in this country of the Scottish verdict of "not proven," I would have to vote to acquit Hauptmann. But I certainly am not ready to convict Lindbergh.

What Can You Do With the Facts?

All of this has been an interesting journey through historic crime. If you want to be a crime writer, whether you are writing fiction or nonfiction, it is important to be aware of what is happening in the real world and what is being said about what is happening. But what, ultimately, does all this have to do with you?

Myriads of writers have deliberately taken real cases and fictionalized them, slightly or very heavily. Myriads of other writers have filled that computer we all keep inside our skulls with true crime, so that when they are ready to plan a book, they are ready to write out an idea.

Amateur detectives *do* solve real cases. Some of them are minor cases, important only to the detective and a few relatives and/or close friends; some are cases of nationwide or worldwide importance. Some of them are historical cases; some are cases happening in the here and now. What can *your* amateur detective do?

Just about whatever you want him or her to do. Keep in mind the motto that opens the television show "X-Files" every week: The truth is out there.

Let your detective find it. He or she will be doing no more, and no less, than other real and fictional amateurs have done.

T E N

EXERCISE: CREATING AN AMATEUR DETECTIVE

This is an exercise Anne Wingate has used in the classroom and when speaking to small groups of writers:

First, get out a piece of paper. Let's invent an amateur sleuth. Where do we start?

Well, where do you start when you meet a real person? Is this person male or female? (Usually, though not always, you can tell at a glance!)

What is this person's racial and ethnic background?

What is this person's religion? Sometimes that is important, sometimes it isn't, but you need to know just in case it turns out to be important.

What is this person's occupation? Obviously he or she is not a professional detective, because we're specifically thinking about amateurs here. But as you learned earlier in the book, an amateur detective can have just about any profession you can possibly think of and probably a few you can't. (We're constantly surprised.)

For this exercise, the character is an undertaker. I can't think of a detective story featuring an undertaker. Most people think it's a rather loathsome occupation, but consider what a mess the world might be in if we didn't have any undertakers.

A male undertaker or a female one? Let's make it a male. Those dead bodies can get pretty heavy to haul around. (Elaine would have gone the distaff route, but maybe next time.)

Okay, we have a male undertaker. I think he's—what? He's a Chinese-American Presbyterian and his name is Henry Song.

Can you see Henry Song yet?

Then let's give him some physical characteristics. Henry is about forty-five. He has black hair and brown eyes. He's about five feet, seven inches tall, and he's a little bit chubby. Not very chubby, just a little bit. When he's on duty, he tries to look very solemn, but on his own time he's a cheerful sort of person. His hobbies are fishing and calligraphy. Not Chinese calligraphy; he's a fifth-generation American and doesn't speak Chinese. But somebody gave him a calligraphy kit as a Christmas present and he got interested in it. Now he does calligraphy for all his friends. He's not too crazy about computers because computers can do calligraphy, too, but he says computer calligraphy doesn't have any soul to it.

Is he married?

I don't think he is.

I think he lives in San Francisco. Is he gay?

I don't know. Neither does anybody else. Henry won't tell and keeps his social life and his business life strictly separate.

Okay, so what kind of cases does Henry get mixed up in?

There's a sort of convention (about seventy years ago, one group of mystery writers went so far as to codify it) that the only crime worthy of a complete novel is murder. That's not true, of course. Dorothy L. Sayers' classic, *Gaudy Night*, contains no actual completed crimes of any more importance than malicious mischief and vandalism, though there are a couple of attempted murders. But I think Henry will get mixed up in a murder.

Hey, there's a book title. *Mixed Up in Murder.* Maybe that's the title of the book we're writing about Henry.

So, how does Henry Song get mixed up in murder?

Well, what does an undertaker do? One of the things he does is go, or send his assistant, to collect dead bodies that aren't going to be autopsied and take them back to the funeral home for preparation for burial. What's involved in that preparation? A lot of things. Go ask your friendly neighborhood undertaker if you really want to know. He or she will probably show you, if you ask nicely enough and have a terribly strong stomach.

So, Henry gets called to pick up this body in Chinatown. The police are already through at the scene. They've released the body to the family, and the family is releasing the body to Henry.

The corpse, who in life was named Edward Li and ran a high-class pawnshop, was about eighty-three years old, was known to have severe heart trouble and had been to the doctor only two days before he died. Everything the police have seen has tended to confirm a heart attack as the cause of death. There's nothing suspicious at all.

The only problem is when Henry gets the body, he finds a depressed skull fracture.

Oops! Whoever put that skull fracture there wasn't thinking about undertakers. There is a law that no bodies can be buried in San Francisco; they can be cremated or shipped somewhere out of the city limits for burial. Most of the family wants him cremated but his oldest daughter, as executor of his estate, has the final say and she insists on burial. This means embalming because a body cannot be shipped anywhere without being embalmed.

Henry calls the police officer who went to the scene and the officer never calls back.

Henry calls this police detective he knows, one Sarah Fleming, and Sarah first gets very interested. Then she calls Henry back and says she's talked to her superior and she's been told to lay off the case. Mr. Li died of a heart attack, and that's official.

(There's a game we used to play in the car on long trips. One person starts a story and then, at a critical spot, tosses the story to the next person to continue.)

Anne to Elaine: It's all yours. Who put the skull fracture in Mr. Li's head? Why did they do it? Was it a personal kill? Somebody in his family, maybe? Or did it have something to do with his business as a pawnbroker? Why is the police department so strangely uninterested? How does Henry find out?

Whose toes does he step on in the process?

I can hear your voices now: But this isn't how to write a mystery! It's never a committee effort! Oh, no? In my experience if the writer has any family or friends, writing a mystery is ultimately a committee effort. You go around screaming and tearing your hair—"I've got my character painted into the corner and I haven't the slightest idea how to get him out!"—and somebody around you makes a useful suggestion.

Okay, Elaine. Pick up the ball and run with it.

(Elaine is going to write the next section of this story, and then we're handing it over to you to finish.)

So, let's see . . .

Henry was on his second cup of steaming oolong tea when he realized why Mr. Li looked so familiar to him. His pawnshop was situated right next to Henry's favorite Chinese restaurant. Mr. Li had a habit of sitting in the rocking chair that was visible courtesy of the shop's large front window.

Henry stared into the tea cup and concentrated; he was able to visualize the window. Very elegant both in its valuable contents and the actual window design. The glass was etched by gold swirls and words both in calligraphic Chinese characters and their corresponding English translation. Henry wondered if the old gentleman was another calligrapher like himself.

In Henry's mind, the answer was yes. And that made Mr. Li more than just a body to be embalmed; it made him an artist and a scholar. With a sigh, Henry put the tea cup down on the sideboard in the upstairs kitchen and was just about to head back downstairs to the mortuary when the telephone rang. He looked at the large desk phone that seemed to fill the top of the counter and noticed it was one of his business lines.

Henry answered in his most professional tone and was greeted by the lyrical voice of Kate Li. She told him she was heading over with a burial outfit for her father and wanted to check and make sure Henry would be there. He said he'd be glad to receive her and they needed to discuss a few other issues.

Henry also took note that his other business phone line was now ringing. Kate Li said she'd be there in about fifteen minutes. After saying good-bye, Henry clicked over to the second line and was greeted by another lyrical voice (this one slightly higher in tone) saying she was Kate Li. This Kate Li said she was on her way over with a burial outfit for her father and wanted to make sure Henry was going to be there.

Henry's interest was piqued to say the least. He told this Kate Li that another patron was on her way over, so if she could arrive in an hour they would have privacy to talk about other burial matters. She agreed.

Henry stared at the phone for a full minute after he'd hung up the receiver. Now he had one dead body with a bashed skull, and two women saying they were the daughter of the deceased. Maybe it was time to call his police detective friend, Sarah Fleming, again. Instead, Henry decided to try the built-in Caller ID unit that was on the phone. He pulled out the instruction manual from its place in the junk drawer, followed each step carefully and wrote down both numbers that had originated the two calls. At least he was acquiring evidence to show Sarah.

On his way down to the basement workroom, Henry tried to remember if he'd ever seen Mr. Li's daughter in the shop. No. Only Mr. Li's face was familiar. Henry automatically straightened a series of calligraphy Chinese symbols he'd mounted on the staircase wall as he waddled down the steps.

He often congratulated himself on finding this particular building. He had been able to have a lovely, roomy apartment built in the attic's double shed dormer. The main house had been redesigned to hold two large elegant viewing rooms off the center foyer, with a casket display area and business office that was not visible by the public. Henry's actual workroom, where he did his embalming, was down another set of stairs in what was a half-cellar area, which provided a hearse-accessible backdoor for discreet deliveries.

Henry was halfway down that set of stairs when he thought he heard something. Rushing, he pushed open the workroom door just as someone was closing the back door. Henry trotted quickly to pull the heavy, steel-framed door open, but no one was visible; only the sound of running hard-soled shoes could be heard.

Henry slammed the door closed and checked twice to make sure the dead bolt was securely in place. This was the first time during his ten years in business that anyone had dared enter the workroom.

Maybe it was just a homeless person? Or a teenager looking for a place to do drugs? Henry muttered to himself as he shrugged off a warning chill, but when he turned around and focused on the body of Mr. Li, he let out an audible gasp!

There was the late, officially declared heart attack victim, Mr. Li, lying half off/half on a stainless steel table with his clothes literally in shreds. Henry hadn't even started embalming work on Mr. Li. And now this!

Someone was obviously looking for something. But what? Henry returned Mr. Li to a less haphazard position on the table, then carefully removed the ripped clothing. First came the sweater, shirt and pants, then the undergarments. After Henry was finished, he placed a clean white sheet over the corpse.

Then he took his time examining the shredded clothing. He checked pockets, inseams, pant cuffs; even the oversized buttons of the sweater were inspected. Henry found nothing. And from the hasty attempt made by the intruder, he hadn't found what he was looking for either.

Henry was thoughtful for a moment. If *something* wasn't hidden in Mr. Li's clothing, where else could it be? Henry checked his watch. Number one daughter was due to arrive in five minutes. He was anxious to meet her and see what she had to say.

Then would come the second Kate Li. Henry was very anxious to see what this young woman would be like and what she would have to say.

The first Kate Li arrived right on schedule and Henry ushered her into his upstairs office. She was attractive with her long black hair in a neat bun, was in her thirties and wore a dark blue business suit. Kate didn't seem upset about her father's death. In fact, she said they'd expected as much since she'd talked with his doctor a few days before.

"His heart was very weak, Mr. Song. I think he welcomed this rest. He had been very upset for the last three days but wouldn't talk about why." She spoke softly. Kate pulled open a small suitcase she'd brought. "I'd like him buried in this traditional long blue gown."

Henry nodded. He spoke to her gently as they discussed

coffins and how she wanted the wake to proceed. "Is there anything else?" He inquired. She shook her head and sighed. He walked her to the door.

Henry checked his watch and saw that there was a good half hour before the second Kate Li would arrive. That gave him more than enough time to rummage through his newspaper recycling bin. Luckily, he hadn't put the papers out and decided to follow-up on a hunch.

Ten minutes later, Henry found what he'd been looking for. An article in the newspaper about a jewelry store robbery and the thieves taking only one item—a two-karat pigeon-blood ruby that was valued at half a million dollars. The jewelry store had been across the street from Mr. Li's pawnshop.

The doorbell sounded, and Henry went down to let in the second Kate Li. She could have been a mirror image of the first woman, except her hair was long on her shoulders and she was wearing a brown trouser suit. This Kate, too, was softly spoken.

"I brought a black suit for my father to be buried in. He was quite modern as you know."

Henry, again, pulled out his brochures and Kate Li chose her father's coffin and told him how she wanted the wake conducted. When she left, Henry checked the kitchen clock and reached for the phone to call Sarah Fleming. This time, Sarah didn't give him the brush-off. She listened when Henry said he could tell her who had killed Mr. Li and said she would be there in five minutes.

Okay. Which daughter is the real Kate Li? If the ruby wasn't in Mr. Li's clothing, is it inside Mr. Li? How did the old man get involved with thieves? Was he murdered or was the head gash just the result of a fall after having a heart attack? Does calligraphy have anything to do with anything?

Can't you just see Miss Jane Marple sitting and smiling over this case? Then she'd begin to nod as her great intellect took over and came to the correct conclusion over who killed Mr. Li and what happened to the ruby. Now it's your turn to start creating your version of this amateur sleuth novel by using the information in this book. If you need further assistance with this case, please write Anne Wingate, ask to go for a ride in her car and continue this game!

Bibliography

Books

Archer, Fred. *Crime and the Psychic World.* New York: Morrow, 1969.

Bassiouni, M. Cherif. *Citizen's Arrest: The Law of Arrest, Search and Seizure for Private Citizens and Private Police.* Springfield, Ill.: Charles C. Thomas, 1977.

Bulgatz, Joseph. *Ponzi Schemes, Invaders From Mars, & More Extraordinary Popular Delusions and the Madness of Crowds.* New York: Harmony Books, 1992.

Carr, John Dickson. *The Blind Barber.* 1934. Reprint. New York: Harper, 1990.

Charteris, Leslie. *The Man Who Was Clever.* 1930. Reprinted in *The Saint: Five Complete Novels.* New York: Avenel, 1983.

Durant, Will and Ariel. *The Age of Voltaire.* Vol. 9. Simon and Schuster: 1965.

Egan, Lesley (pseudonym: Elizabeth Linington). *Look Back on Death.* New York: Doubleday, 1978.

Fawcett, Lawrence and Barry J. Greenwood. *Clear Intent: The Government Coverup of the UFO Experience.* Englewood Cliffs, NJ: Prentice-Hall, 1984.

Goodman, Jonathan, ed. *The Art of Murder.* New York: Carol Publishing Group, 1992.

–. *Lady Killers: Famous Woman Murderers.* New York: Citadel, 1990.

–. *Medical Murders.* New York: Carol Publishing Group, 1992.

Gorman, Ed, Martin Greenberg, Larry Segriff with Jon L. Breen. *The Fine Art of Murder: The Mystery Reader's Indispensable Companion.* New York: Caroll & Graf, 1993.

Heising, Willetta L. *Detecting Women: A Reader's Guide and Checklist for Mystery Series Written by Women.* Dearborn, MI: Purple Moon Press, 1994.

Jones, Richard Glyn, ed. *Solved! Famous Mystery Writers on Classic True Crime Case.* New York: Peter Bedrick Books, 1987.

–. *Unsolved! Classic True Murder Cases.* New York: Peter Bedrick Books, 1987.

Kennedy, Ludovic. *The Airman and the Carpenter: The Lindbergh Kidnapping and the Framing of Richard Hauptmann.* New York: Viking, 1985.

la Cour, Tage and Harald Mogensen. *The Murder Book.* New York: Herder and Herder, 1971.

LeBlanc, Maurice. *The Extraordinary Adventures of Arsene Lupin, Gentleman-Burglar.* 1910. Reprint. New York: Dover Publications, 1977.

Lockridge, Frances and Richard. *The Norths Meet Murder.* 1940. Reprint. New York: World, 1946.

McGarvey, Robert and Elise Caitlin. *The Complete Spy: An Insider's Guide to the Latest in High-Tech Espionage & Equipment.* New York: Perigee, 1983.

Nash, Jay Robert. *The Encyclopedia of World Crime: Criminal Justice, Criminology and Law Enforcement.* 6 vols. Wilmette, IL: CrimeBooks, Inc., 1990.

Packard, Frank L. *The Further Adventures of Jimmie Dale.* New York: Burt, 1919.

Pankau, Edmund J. *Check It Out: A Top Investigator Show You How to Find Out Practically Anything About Anybody in Your Life.* Chicago: Contemporary Books, 1992.

Poe, Edgar Allan. *Complete Stories and Poems of Edgar Allan Poe.* New York: Doubleday & Company, 1966.

Rinehart, Mary Roberts. *Miss Pinkerton: Adventures of a Nurse Detective.* 1914, 1932, 1942. Reprint. New York: Rinehart, 1959.

Sayers, Dorothy L. *Gaudy Night.* 1936. Reprint. New York: HarperCollins Publishers, 1993.

–. *Whose Body?* 1923. Reprint. New York: HarperCollins Publishers, 1993.

Slfakis, Carl. *The Encyclopedia of American Crime.* New York: Facts on File, 1982.

Steinbrunner, Chris and Otto Penzler. *Encyclopedia of Mystery & Detection.* New York: McGraw-Hill, 1976.

Tillman, Norma Jott. *How to Find Almost Anyone, Anywhere.* Nashville: Rutledge Hill, 1994.

Waller, George. *Kidnap: The Story of the Lindbergh Case.* New York: Dial, 1961.

Weider, Ben and David Hapgood. *The Murder of Napoleon.* New York: Congden, 1982.

Yallop, David A. *In God's Name: An Investigation Into the Murder of Pope John Paul I.* New York: Bantam, 1984.

Magazine Articles

"@ Work With Gina Smith." *Glamour* (February 1996).

Bailey, Janet. "When in Doubt, Check'em Out - How to Be Your Own Private Eye." *Know How* (Premier Issue 1995).

Brown, Marshall J. "Husband Murders Wife Disarmed by Police." *Women & Guns*, Vol. 6, no. 10 (November 1994): 10ff.

Clavin, Thomas. "Is Your Boss Spying on You?" *Ladies Home Journal* (July 1995).

Cooper, Joel. "Doctor It Up on the Web." *Online Access* (October 1995): 26-27.

"Determining Lies Can Be Difficult." *USA Today: The Magazine of the American Scene* Vol. 122, Is. 2599 (April 1995).

Duncan, Lois. "Can Psychics Solve Crimes?" *Woman's Day* (April 1, 1992): 30ff.

"Editor's Choice." *Online Access* (October 1995).

"Fast Forward to the Future." *Family Circle* (January 9, 1996).

Fisher, David. "Evidence That Does Not Lie." Condensed from *Hard Evidence* in *Reader's Digest.* Date unavailable.

Forsythe, Clover with Mary Ellin Barrett. "I Brought My Sister's Attackers to Justice." *McCall's* (November 1994): 106ff.

Foster, D. Glenn and Mary Marshall. "How to Tell When a Person Is Lying." *Good Housekeeping*, Vol. 218, no. 6 (June 1994): 46-48.

Gottlieb, Anne. "Five Ways to Conquer Your Fear." *McCall's* (July 1995).

"Hacker Quacks." *Men's Health* (January/February 1996).

Hershkowitz, Sherry. "Bells and Whistles, Which Self-Protection Devices Do You Really Need?" *Know How* (Premier Issue 1995).

Hollander, Dory Ph.D. "Is He Telling You the Truth?" *Good Housekeeping* (March 1996).

"How to Catch a Liar in the Act." *Glamour* (date unavailable).

"How to Spot a Liar." *First for Women* (February 19, 1996).

"Insites." *PC Computing* (March 1996).

"I Spy." *Glamour* (date unavailable).

Jatras, Todd. "Virtually Literature." *The San Francisco Review of Books* (January/February 1996).

Kaufman, Margo. "What Eavesdroppers Know (and You Should Learn)." *Redbook* (May 1995).

Lesser, Elizabeth. "How Do You Coax a Confession Out of Someone?" *Know How* (Premier Issue 1995).

Pepper, Jon. "Pagers Come of Age." *Home Office Computing* (January 1996): 38-41.

Rafkin, Louise. "The New Rules for Street Smarts." *Ladies Home Journal* (July 1995).

Rash, Wayne Jr. "Interstate Caller ID Helps Entrepreneurs." *Home Office Computing* (March 1995).

–."Hold Your Calls." *Home Office Computing* (March 1995): 100-106.

"Realities Resources: Checking a Doctor's Credentials." *Glamour* (date unavailable).

"Realities Resources: Five Steps to Take if You're Worried About Being Stalked." *Glamour* (June 1994).

"Realities Resources: New Ways to Stop Phone Harassment." *Glamour* (November 1994).

Reibstein, Larry, Michael Isikoff, Mark Hoseball. "The Prying Game Under New Rules." *Newsweek* (September 5, 1994).

Sanborn, Margaret. "A Chronic Fatigue Epic: Journalist-Sufferer Writes Saga for Crown." *Publisher's Weekly* (December 4, 1995). Reprint. *The CFIDS Chronicle*, Vol. 9, no. 1 (Winter 1990): 5-6.

Saunders, Debra J. "I Spy Online." *Home Office Computing* (June 1995).

"Services to Make Your Phone Do Just About Anything." *Good Housekeeping* (July 1995): 161.

Tanzer, Marc. "Thwarting the Techno-Spy." *SKY* (September 1994): 134-142.

Tenopir, Carol. "Online Databases." *Library Journal* (July 1994).

"Tips to Help Detect Lying." *USA Today* Vol. 123, Is. 2591 (August 1994).

Updegrave, Walter L. "You're Safer Than You Think." *Money* (June 1994).

"Upfront." *Home Office Computing* (November 1995): 24.

"Upfront." *Home Office Computing* (January 1996): 17.

Virginia Commonwealth University. *Library Online*, Vol. 9, no. 1 (Fall 1995).

Wallechinsky, David. "Be at Home on the Internet." *Parade* (November 19, 1995).

"Web Watch." *Publishers Weekly* (January 22, 1996).

"What Police Are Saying." *Parade* (November 26, 1995).

Will, George F. "Are We 'A Nation of Cowards'?" *Newsweek* (November 15, 1993): 92.

Newspapers and Newsletters

Alexander, Jack. "Dad's Faith Digs up New Dirt on Daughter's 1978 Murder!" *Weekly World News* (April 4, 1995): 2.

–. " 'I Told You So!' Murder Victim Found EXACTLY Where Psychic Predicted—5 Years Ago." *Weekly World News* (May 19, 1995).

"Blake Patterson's UnDirectory." *New York Daily News* (date unavailable).

Dexter, Beatrice. "Rape Victim Places Personals Ad to Catch Her Attacker!" *National Enquirer* (date unavailable).

Dudman, Graham. "Mom Turns Private Eye in 20-year Hunt for Missing Daughter." *Star* (January 2, 1996).

Great Lakes Bookseller Newsletter, Vol. 8, no. 1 (March 1996).

–.Vol. 7, no. 5.

Hughes, David T. "Enter the Net." *Fairfax Journal* (November 27, 1995).

–. "Trying to Regulate the Internet." *Fairfax Journal* (February 12, 1996).

Kilman, Todd. "The New Information Desk." Fast Forward. *Washington Post* (July 1995).

Krewatch, Mark. "Detective Hotline Dials for Clues." *Centre View* (May 19, 1994): 28.

McNichol, Tom. "Secret Weapons." *USA Weekend* (December 29-31, 1995): cover story.

Quinn, Tom. "Parents Track Down, Turn in Man Who Flashed Teen Daughter." *Salt Lake Tribune* (January 8, 1995).

–. "Woman Tracks Down Identity of Former Houseguest Who Came Back to Steal." *Salt Lake Tribune* (February 7, 1996): B3.

Rahn, B.J. Professor. "Murder Is Academic—The Teaching and Criticism of Crime Fiction on Campus." Hunter College. Vol. 3. (November 1995).

"Scoop on Your Broker." Dow Jones News Service (date not shown).

The Bulldog. A newsletter from Parents Against Corruption & Coverup, 13456 Muirkirk Lane, Herndon, VA 22071. (703) 435-3112. Vol. 2, no. 3 (Fall 1995).

Washington Post. "Advent of the Two-Way Pager." (November 14, 1994).

–. "Caller ID Is Going the Distance." (December 4, 1995).

–. "Censors Beware: It's Difficult to Control Information on the 'Net." WashTech (February 12, 1996).

–. "Cyberporn Debate Goes International." WashTech (January 1, 1996).

–. "FBI Data Show 12 Percent Decline in Murder, Biggest Drop in Decades." Associated Press (December 18, 1995).

–. "FBI Lab Audit Finds Some Discrepancies." (September 15, 1995).

–. "FCC Wireless Applications Up." Business Notes (December 29, 1995).

–. "For Many in North Philadelphia, Police Corruption Is No Surprise." (October 5, 1995).

–. "Human Error Cited on Simpson Blood." (September 14, 1995).

–. "In Silver Spring, the Public Can Log On to the Police Log." (May 23, 1994).

–. "Internet's Reach in Society Grows, Survey Finds." (October 31, 1995).

–. "Paging Takes a New Direction." (October 2, 1995).

–. "Pixels at an Exhibition." (January 19, 1996).

–. "Police Search of AOL Files Divides the On-Line World." (January 26, 1996).

–. "SEC Offers Corporate Data On-Line at No Cost to Public." (September

29, 1995).
–. "Surfing Blind." Fast Forward (January 1996).
–. "Taking to the Road With Help From the World Wide Web." (September 25, 1995).
–. "The Phone Exchange." Business Notes (July 24, 1995).
–. "Undercover on the Dark Side of Cyberspace." (January 2, 1996).
–. "Who Was That Masked Cybershopper?" (February 2, 1996).

Government and Consumer Pamphlets

Bell Atlantic. Various consumer information material.
Government of Canada. *Info Sources: Personal Information Request Form.* Ottawa: Minister of Supply and Services (1995).
–. *The Privacy Act.* Ottawa: Minister of Supply and Services (1995).
–. *Privacy Commissioner's Annual Report 1994-1995.* Ottawa: Canada Communications Group (1995).
Leiter, Richard. *National Survey of State Laws.* Washington, D.C.: Gale Research (1993).
U.S. Department of Justice. *Freedom of Information Act Guide & Privacy Act Overview.* Washington, D.C.: U.S. Government Printing Office (1993).
U.S. Department of the Treasury, Bureau of Alcohol, Tobacco and Firearms. *Firearms State Laws and Published Ordinances.* Washington, D.C.: U.S. Government Printing Office (1994 and 1996).

Miscellaneous

1-800-HI-HELLO, Direct. HelloHint No. 5. Page 45.
"CBS Evening News," *Eye on America: Jim McClosky, True to Life Amateur Detective.* (November 21, 1995).
Microsoft Bookshelf '95. CD-Rom. Multimedia Reference Library.
Microsoft Encarta '95. CD-Rom. The Complete Interactive Multi-Media Encyclopedia.
SpyTech Store, 2144 Yonge Street, Toronto, Ontario M4S 2A8, Canada. Phone: 416-482-8588.

Index

Buell, Martin, 21
Bulldog Drummond, 14
Bunn, Smiler, 13
Burke, Jan, 34
Burkett, Tommy, 193-195
Burns, Carl, 36
Butterworth, Amelia, 8

Cadfael, Brother, 44
Cain, Jenny, 32
Caliban, Cat, 41
California, 76, 79, 103, 119, 125
  Brady Law, 125
  citizen's arrest, 125
Callihan, Ray, 189, 195
Canada, 165-167, 169, 182-185
Cannell, Dorothy, 33, 48
Carlisle, Kenneth, 16
Carlson, P.M., 36
Carnacki, 10
Carne, Simon, 13
Carr, John Dickson, 16, 18
Casey, Jack "Flashgun," 25
Cates, Molly, 34
Caudwell, Sarah, 34
Cellini, Dr. Emmanuel, 19
Chambrun, Pierre, 9, 10
Chapman, Olivia, 48
Charles, Edwina, 43
Charles, Kate, 34
Charles, Nick and Nora, 22
Charteris, Leslie, 14
Chase, Elizabeth, 43
Chesterton, G.K., 21
Chizzit, Emma, 42
Christie, Dame Agatha, 16, 22, 31, 32,
  53, 70
Churchill, Jill, 48
Citizen's arrest, 116-117, 118. *See also*
  the individual states.
Clark, Carolyn Chambers, 35
Clay, Colonel, 13
Clear intent 170, 171
Cleary, Melissa, 49
Cleek, Hamilton, 13
Cleeves, Ann, 40
Clerk, court, 72
  county, 73, 76
Clively, Miranda and Clare, 44
Clunk, Joshua, 11
Cobb, Matt, 35
Coben, Harlan, 37
Cody, Liza, 48
Coel, Margaret, 46
Colorado, 39, 42, 79, 125-126
  Brady Law, 126

citizen's arrest, 126
Conant, Susan, 49
Confession, 58
Connecticut, 79, 95, 126, 127
  Brady Law, 126
  citizen's arrest, 126
Contact guides, 81
Cooper, Iris, 45
Cooper, Susan Rogers, 34
Cork, Montague, 26, 35
Cornwell, Patricia, 35
Court
  civil, 72-74, 178
  criminal, 71-73, 88, 178
  family, 73
  federal district, 73, 74
  municipal, 72
  probate, 73, 76
Court of Last Resort, 188
Coxe, George H., 25
Craig, Melissa, 34
Crane, Hamilton, 36
Cranston, Lamont, 15
Creasy, John, 15, 19
Crespi, Camilla, 39
Crider, Bill, 36, 38
Criminal
  code, 121, 133, 165, 166
  procedure, 159
  record, 122, 133, 165, 166
Crispin, Edmund, 25
Crook, Arthur, 12
Cross, Amanda, 36
Crowleigh, Ann, 44
Crum, Laura, 36
Crusoe, Edwina, 35

da Silva, Jane, 41
Daheim, Mary, 34, 39
Dallas, Eve, 49
Dalrymple, Daisy, 45
Daly, Elizabeth, 20
Dams, Jeanne M., 42
Danforth, Abigail Patience, 45
Dann, Peaches, 41
Darcy, Tess, 39
Dare, Susan, 20
Darling, Annie Laurance, 31
Davidson, Diane Mott, 39
Davis, Dorothy Salisbury, 40
Davis, Shelley, 172
de Coventry, Dowager Countess, 45
Deadly force, 151, 152
DeAndrea, William L., 35
Dee, Judge, 12
Delaware, 36, 79, 127